"Love knows no bounds."

- Unknown

"Space knows no gender."

- Kevin Sawyer

"I do for all."

- U.S. Supreme Court

ACKNOWLEDGMENTS

GROUND CONTROL

Thank you, Jeff, for putting up with all the mornings, nights, and weekends I spent working on this project, for marrying me, and most of all, for inspiring this and many other realms of creativity.

Thank you to my parents, Marilee and Don, for the love, support, and encouragement from my childhood to my marriage to all the creative paths ahead. Thank you to Jeff's parents, Carolyn and Norm, for raising one hell of a son and always encouraging us to find our next adventure together.

Thank you, Carla Corcoran, for galvanizing so many mantras used throughout the book, and for your support and love since the great days of our college youth.

Thank you, Jenn Nichols, for putting up with Jeff all these years, for becoming one of my dearest friends, and for testing the crap out of the worksheets.

Thank you, Skye Poole, for being one of the first people to give unabashed, unfiltered feedback, even when weddings were the furthest thing from your mind.

Thank you, Kim Pfluger, for all your support, feedback, and for always being my partner in crime when it comes to incessantly loving all that is space.

R+D DECK

To all the early survey-takers and usability testers — this workbook would not be in such a refined state were it not for all of you! Thank you Emily Arkin, Ken Burke, Angela Candelario, Jenna Cappello, Megan Hartman, TJ Jordan, Kate Katin, Erin Krajewski, Supicha Kridaratikorn, Amanda Lovelee, Jay Magrisso, Melissa Misicka, Biz Murray, Jenn Nolte, Mike Smith, Kelly Turner, Jennifer Turpin, and Rose Yaksic.

Thank you to NASA's Kennedy Space Center and the Cambridge Antique Market for providing a dearth of visual inspiration, research, and discovery.

WEDDING INDUSTRY FLIGHT DECK

Thank you, Megan Finley and the OffbeatBride.com crew, for publishing my work and sharing it with a community so near and dear to my heart.

Thank you to OffbeatBride.com commenters Hannah, Heather, pinkhairerin, KathyRo, Jessica, Amanda, KiusLady Tribesmaid, Tribesmate Nic, and PersephoneUnderground. That small bit of back and forth proved this was an idea worth chasing.

Thank you to Nicole, Venetia, Jenna, and Tara of the Greater Boston Wedding Professionals Meetup. Your unfettered enthusiasm and encouragement kept my oxygen levels stable at the halfway point.

Thank you, Sandra Costello, for truly being one of the greatest photographers and people I've ever had the pleasure of working with. Your nonstop sparkle is what keeps so many couples-to-be intact on the big day. In addition, thanks for being an early vetting voice when AstroWed was just an infant of an idea.

LIFTOFF

Thank you to the hosts of Shameless Book Marketing for Indie Authors, Elaine Orabona Foster and Joe Foster. Your feedback, energy, and knowledge was exactly what I needed at a time when uncertainty was at its peak — I am forever grateful.

Thank you, Reedsy, for creating the opportunity to find the perfect editor, and for sharing our editing process with the Reedsy community.

And finally, thank you, Rachel Small, for being the best damn editor I could have hoped for — I've never collaborated or laughed this much across continents. We can move Martian mountains together, I'm sure of it!

CONTENTS

A LETTER TO YOU,
THE COUPLE-TO-BE:

AstroWed grew out of weekly blog posts on the successes, failures, and frustrations of wedding planning. Posts such as "How to shop for a wedding dress like a software engineer" were featured on OffbeatBride.com, so I quickly began to see there was a need for more: More room for couples to be themselves. More than the checkboxes the wedding industry creates. More than the stereotypical landscape of bride-only products, where one can rarely find a helpful tool for nontraditional brides and grooms and LGBTQ couples. In short, I created AstroWed to help you — and to help the thousands of other couples-to-be who just want a wedding-planning tool that feels like an "us" thing rather than a "person you're supposed to be" thing.

AstroWed doesn't look like other wedding-planning workbooks for a reason. It's not about overwhelming checklists of things you're supposed to do. It's not about the traditions of our parents and their parents' parents. It's not about gender, Tiffany blue, or curly girly bullshit. *AstroWed* is about *how* you'll cross off to-dos, knowing all along they're the to-dos that matter to YOU. It's about creating a **space** for you and your partner. It's also about acknowledging the **universe** in which you'll make tons of decisions (with the least amount of stress possible) leading up to the moment where you both say, "I do."

Bottom line: wedding planning is hard. AstroWed is here to make it a little easier — without social pressure.

The AstroWed framework stems from my personal experiences in planning my own wedding and doing a shit ton of project management over the years. But don't worry. I've worked tirelessly to remove the boring, awful stuff and bring in the **rocket-boosting fuel** we all need to get us from "Will you marry me?" to "I do."

I hope this method of checking off those to-dos will make your big day the best damn day of your life. You're getting married! To the person you love! **Make some space for an out-of-this-world wedding — YOUR WEDDING!**

Thank you. Now let's kick some serious wedding-planning ass, shall we?

*Note: This is the first edition of AstroWed. I'm excited for the honest feedback, the conversations, and, if all goes well, the effect AstroWed will have on a severely traditional industry. While the concepts and rough drafts were tested with couples of all kinds, it's still not enough. So if you'd like to help shape the next edition, head to the contact form on **Astro-Wed.com**. I'd love to hear your stories and see how you made the big day all about you and your partner. Most of all, if you used the AstroWed framework, I'd love to hear feedback on what worked and what didn't. Please share!*

INTRODUCING SANITY!

Brought to you by AstroWed.

Everyone says wedding planning is monstrously stressful, but how stressful is it really, and how can we prevent it?

For starters, did you know that on a list of 43 life events, participants ranked "marriage" as the seventh most stressful?[1] On the Holmes and Rahe Stress Scale, getting married is:

- More than twice as stressful as moving
- More stressful than getting fired
- More stressful than the death of a close friend!

Holy shit. Just tell your fiancé to return that ring and go hug your closest friend. Maybe leave your fiancé and move in with your friend . . .

No, no, wait, come back!

Don't give up just yet. All of us married folk (newlyweds and oldyweds) promise it's worth it, really! There just happens to be a big bucket of reality waiting on the other side of the love rainbow.

During the average one-year engagement, people organizing their own weddings spend anywhere from 100 to 150 hours on the task.[2] It's like a part-time job!

And, a recent discovery in relationship science states that we have the ability to raise stress levels in our partners.[3] Are you surprised? Have you met your parents? I'm not surprised either.

If you hear your inner "'Zilla" (an alien-induced neurological condition; for more information, see page 36) screeching in the distance, know that your stress level can affect the physical well-being of your partner.

Okay, enough with the gloom and doom.

Even if you don't plan on wearing white, there's a way to find the bright happy light in all of this madness. The goal with wedding planning is to stay positive, right? If you can look at the silver lining (marrying that beautiful soul who sits across the dinner table), chances are your big day will be fulfilling rather than frustrating.

Right, uh-huh. Stay positive. If it's more stressful than getting fired, how the hell are you supposed keep a good attitude about this whole endeavor?

It's simple. Write down what you do and don't want and then make a decision. Embrace the joy of decision-making. Embrace that this is YOUR universe. This is about YOU TWO. Own it. Decide. Celebrate.

That's it?

Blogger Eric Barker (author of *Barking Up The Wrong Tree*) said it best: "Staying positive isn't always easy but more and more research is showing that just a little writing can make a big difference."[4]

Barker has written a number of articles on this subject, as well as on reducing worry and quelling fears, and he has "expert insight on how to be awesome at life." Many of these articles essentially boil down to the health benefits of:

- Writing down your concerns
- Writing down your progress
- Writing down your goals
- Writing about your relationship
- Writing down the good things that happen to you[5]

AstroWed is here to get the brain-sucking aliens out of your head and put them to work on paper.

This is YOUR UNIVERSE. You have goals, your partner does too. If you talk about them and write them down, chances are you can fight the good fight together and make those decisions confidently, with as little stress as possible.

1. Thomas H. Holmes and Richard H. Rahe, "The Social Readjustment Rating Scale," *Journal of Psychosomatic Research*, Volume 11, no. 2 (1967): 213–218. 2. Elizabeth Alterman, "Should You Say 'I Do' to a Wedding Planner," CNBC.com, May 7, 2012, http://www.cnbc.com/id/46797144. 3. Oxford University Press USA. "Mortality and blood pressure directly linked to relationship quality." ScienceDaily. ScienceDaily, 7 April 2015, www.sciencedaily.com/releases/2015/04/150407153332.htm. 4. Eric Barker, "Is writing the best way to reduce worry and keep staying positive?" *Barking Up The Wrong Tree* (blog), July 2, 2013, http://www.bakadesuyo.com/2013/07/staying-positive/. 5. Eric Barker, "This One Simple Thing Can Make Your Life Much Better," *Barking Up The Wrong Tree* (blog) July 29, 2013, http://www.bakadesuyo.com/2013/07/personal-writing/.

There's a scientific benefit to decision-making as well. When we make decisions, we create intentions and set goals. This engages our brain positively, minimizing worry and anxiety. Our ability to make decisions also directly affects the part of the brain that controls instinct and mood. The more decisions we make (even if they're super tiny), the quicker we can see a solution the next time a challenge arises. If we decide to write something down, we're practicing decision-making skills without even knowing it. Small actions such as writing down what you like and dislike train the brain to get away from the land of "I DON'T KNOW! I'M SO STRESSED OUT!" and travel to the world of "If we don't like XYZ, let's look at ABC tomorrow."[6]

But what happens when we try too hard to find the perfect pair of shoes to match our big-day outfit? It's scientifically too much, says neuroscientist Alex Korb:

"Trying for the best, instead of good enough, brings too much emotional ventromedial prefrontal activity into the decision-making process. In contrast, recognizing that good enough is good enough activates more dorsolateral prefrontal areas, which helps you feel more in control . . ."[7]

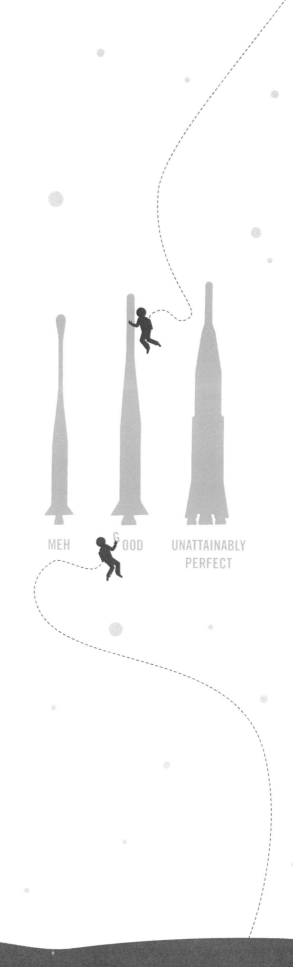

MEH   GOOD   UNATTAINABLY PERFECT

If we constantly try to find the perfect item (especially for the big day), our brain can get emotionally frustrated. This constant state of aggravation also forces our happiness to plummet. That negativity seeps into our search, making each item we pick up seem less and less like the perfect thing. We essentially become blinded by our frustration!

So what's the cure? Set a goal of finding an item that's good enough.

I'm a designer by trade, and "good enough" is something we talk about regularly in software design and development. Much of my experience stems from a variety of different design processes like Lean UX, Agile methods, and prospective hindsight, all of which ultimately drive towards a good-enough product.

The path we take to get to the good-enough decision is challenging. It's fuzzy. It has hills and plateaus. Good-enough needs walls, boundaries, indicators that tell us how little or how much to shoot for to achieve a certain goal. There are SO MANY CHOICES when it comes to planning a wedding — how do you find the boundaries to tell you which way to go?

6. Alex Korb PhD and Daniel J. Siegel MD, *The Upward Spiral: Using Neuroscience to Reverse the Course of Depression, One Small Change at a Time* (New Harbinger Publications, 2015), 95–96. 7. Ibid., 94.

Welcome to AstroWed! YOU MADE IT!
Your journey to wedding-planning sanity begins here.

WHAT IS ASTROWED?

AstroWed is a framework designed to help you make decisions for each item on that overwhelming wedding checklist. Inspired by the journey of planning my own wedding and my work in the tech industry, AstroWed reminds you that this is YOUR WEDDING (and it reminds you often!) while asking you to sort out the stress of every detail with lists of wants and don't wants.

WHAT IS A FRAMEWORK?

A framework is like a blueprint for getting shit done. With just about every task in life, we have a reason, a method, a process to cross it off a to-do list. Think of how you do laundry, run errands, or pack for a trip; I bet there's a special path you take each time and you're fairly comfortable in your methods. Planning my wedding made me second-guess myself more than I would have liked, but in the end, I found solace in my tech methodologies. They helped me pick the right elements for the biggest day of my life.

AstroWed is a framework designed to help you find confidence in each decision, have less stress, and keep those wedded wits intact. Think of it like a sixth sense for sanity — it asks the right questions to lead to an answer YOU feel good about, from venues to outfits to rings. [I was really bad at remembering the big day was OUR day, not anyone else's, and thus I'll be squawking positive words of self-care your way regularly.]

WHO IS ASTROWED FOR?

AstroWed is not just for couples-to-be — it's also a helpful tool for bridal party members and wedding helpers. I bring up "helpers" because it can be difficult to ask for help when this whole wedding-planning thing feels like it lives on your shoulders and your shoulders alone. It doesn't have to! Create a Wedding Day Dream Team made of both bridal party members and talented helpers-at-large. Divide and conquer these wedding to-dos TOGETHER. This is YOUR DAY and you deserve every ounce of aid that others offer.

WHY ASTROWED?

There are more wedding-planning books, websites, and checklists than stars in the sky these days. Most of them are riddled with gender stereotypes and frilly designs and are built for the female bride only — as if SHE is the only one who should do all the work or care the most. This, friends, is bullshit.

If you're a heterosexual couple, what about the groom? Can't he find something for HIM that's not soft-pink and dipped in glitter? What if you're a LGBTQ couple planning the world's most kickass Game of Thrones–themed wedding? How does any of this stereotypical crap apply to you?

In planning my own wedding, I didn't find the traditional wedding tools terribly helpful. Yes, there is loads of content, ideas, and DIY-everything out there, but I had 30+ items on my wedding checklist. I'm an organized, task-driven person, but that list threw me into a panic. I just wanted someone to tell me HOW to choose a dress, HOW to choose my officiant, and HOW to pick the right table favors — without shoving industry trends down my throat. We all know what we like (most of the time!) and I like to be unique, damnit. I didn't want to just tear out a page of the magazine and say, "Ohhhhh that's the one" for every detail. The pressure of it all was ulcer inducing!

In the few moments where my sanity decided to hang around, I tapped into organizational methods I'd learned from working in software design over the years. But the problem with tech-centered methods is that they're made for technical people; at first blush they're pretty dry, unapproachable, and hard to understand. I want to change that, specifically for the process of planning a wedding, with AstroWed.

AstroWed, the Framework

AstroWed breaks down each wedding checklist to-do into twelve parts:

1. **Identity Statement**
2. **Online Research**
3. **Style + Look**
4. **MaCaW!**
5. **Environmental Conditions**
6. **Time Machine: Fail**

7. **Time Machine: Success**
8. **Prototype Time**
9. **Get-Ready List**
10. **Vendor / In-Store Research**
11. **Landing Gear**
12. **COMPLETE!**

Let's take a closer look.

1. IDENTITY STATEMENT

This little fill-in-the-blank helps you focus on what YOU want because remember, this is YOUR day. It allows you to take a first look into your desired results or goals for each wedding to-do through statements that define you and your partner. (Wedding helpers can also use this tool.) Here's how the identity statement is set up:

I am • We are • They are a _____ bride • groom • partner • couple (CIRCLE ONE)
(CIRCLE ONE) ADJECTIVE wedding party member • helper

and need to find a _____ **Reception Venue**
ADJECTIVES CHECKLIST ITEM

that will feel _____
ADJECTIVES, EMOTIONS

and won't _____ or _____ .
UNWANTED RESULT, FEELING UNWANTED RESULT

No, this isn't ninth grade English class all over again — it's your wedding, damnit. Here's an example of my identity statement for our reception venue:

STACEY'S IDENTITY STATEMENT

I am • We are • They are an <u>adventurous, beach-loving</u> bride • groom • partner • couple (CIRCLE ONE)
(CIRCLE ONE) ADJECTIVE wedding party member • helper

and need to find a <u>tropical</u> **Reception Venue**
ADJECTIVES CHECKLIST ITEM

that will feel <u>relaxed yet exotic</u>
ADJECTIVES, EMOTIONS

and won't <u>be too formal</u> or <u>too difficult to manage from afar</u>.
UNWANTED RESULT, FEELING UNWANTED RESULT

Now let's try one together. **Think about your reception venue, whether you've decided on one or not. Write down the first thing that comes to mind.** One key strategy here: don't overthink this exercise! Take a deep breath in, and on the exhale just write down whatever floats into your mind.

YOUR IDENTITY STATEMENT

I am • We are • They are a _____ bride • groom • partner • couple   (CIRCLE ONE)
(CIRCLE ONE)   ADJECTIVE   wedding party member • helper

and need to find a _____ Reception Venue
                                    ADJECTIVES   CHECKLIST ITEM

that will feel _____
                              ADJECTIVES, EMOTIONS

and won't _____ or _____.
              UNWANTED RESULT, FEELING   UNWANTED RESULT

Now, embrace the awkwardness and read it out loud. It's an odd thing to do but trust me, hearing things outside your head that usually live inside makes them attainable, and real.

Some questions for you:

- ❷ If you haven't thought about the reception venue yet, can you envision a few places in your mind?
- ❷ Do you feel like you might have an idea of where to start?
- ❷ If you've already chosen your venue, do you feel better about your choice or worse?
- ❷ Does it match what defines your as well as your partner's goals?

Note: The identity statement is the first step towards AstroWed sanity, inspired by my very own matron of honor, who consistently asked me, "Yes, but is this what YOU want? Is this what both of you want?"

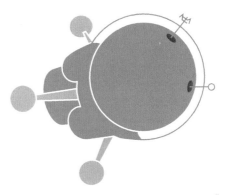

HOW TO USE THIS WORKBOOK

2. ONLINE RESEARCH

Now that you've identified who you are and your reception venue goals, let's visit the most common of research laboratories: the Internet! This chart is a simple place to jot down the sites you've visited and any key takeaways that may narrow down your search. Below is a sample list from our reception venue search.

STACEY'S ONLINE RESEARCH

littlepalmisland.com	Looks amazing, and expensive, worry about activities for kids and families.
postcardinn.com	Everything looks modern & approachable. Also all-inclusive w/marina activities.
hawkscay.com	Another beautiful place with lots of options even for newborns. Looks like a variety of venues on-site too.
hemingwayhome.com	Super cool vibe but everything is à la carte.

Alrighty! Write down the venue websites you've visited and any points of interest that you may want to consider or look at once more. This might be a great time to share your thoughts with your partner or family members if you're looking for a second opinion on what places may be worth visiting.

YOUR ONLINE RESEARCH

IHeartThisWebsiteLikeWhoa.com	Notes on why this website kicks ass for our wedding

3. STYLE + LOOK

For most wedding to-dos, there is a look, a feel, a style that will match the vibe you're trying to create for the big day. After launching your first research journey you may form some solid opinions about what you do and don't want.

When using the Style + Look section, think of the Love and Hate lists as separate buckets. For example, if you love the idea of a tent, you don't have to write down "hotel ballroom" under Hate just because it corresponds. To illustrate a bit further, here's my Style + Look list:

STACEY'S STYLE + LOOK

LOVE		HATE
a good bit of high-end style upon entering		cheap motel-like places
relaxed vacation offerings		college bro-zones
bigger, more expansive places with options		bad food, bad drinks

Now, use the chart below to zero in on styles and looks that YOU love and hate. Write down all the things you love in a reception venue and then list all the things you don't want in a venue. These buckets of "Yay!" and "Ugh" are also really helpful to vendors when you call potential places or look at things on-site. Communication is key! And hey, sharing is caring, even when it's a fact like "I DON'T LIKE YELLOW!" Remember, this is YOUR DAY.

YOUR STYLE + LOOK

LOVE		HATE

4. MaCaW

A macaw is a beautiful bird; a **MaCaW** is a mnemonic device for Must-Could-Won't. And since macaws are from the parrot family, you'll see this symbol throughout the book squawking, "Remember! This is YOUR WEDDING!" The **Must-Could-Won't** chart is one of the cornerstones of AstroWed. It narrows your line of sight, reminding you what you can't live without, what you could have, and what will absolutely not be. Here's my **MaCaW** chart for our reception venue:

STACEY'S MaCaW

MUST	COULD	WON'T
be tropical	be somewhere famous like the Hemingway Home	be a wedding factory
be in the US		be too expensive for guests
be fairly easy to get to	be a private island	be scheduled during spring break or hurricane season
have kid options	be an all-in-one resort	
		be too stressful to plan from afar

The **MaCaW** chart is a close relative of the identity statement, helping you get deeper into your hopes, wishes, and Oh Hell Nos. So, let's go back to the reception venue and apply **MaCaW**. Just like the Style items, the items in this chart don't have to correspond. Think of it as a bucket of Must, a bucket of Could, and a bucket of Won't. Again, relax and **write whatever comes to the front of your mind about your ideal venue. Often your first thought is the strongest of the pack, and thus the right thing to focus on.**

YOUR MaCaW

MUST	COULD	WON'T

A few questions for you:

- ❷ Was there anything in the three columns that surprised you?

- ❷ Were there things you've been thinking about but haven't shared with your partner?

- ❷ Does this help prioritize the qualities you want in your reception venue? Good! It should make it a bit easier to make a final decision, too.

That last question is the true purpose of **MaCaW**. We usually know what we want, but sometimes it's hard to see what might be more important or what qualities outrank others. It's also great to be able to tell any of your vendors right out of the gate, "I'd like to look at something like this but please don't bother showing me anything like that. We've decided it isn't for us." You'll save your own time as well as the vendor's, therefore making the review process a streamlined experience.

5. Environmental Conditions

Everything from the obvious (the venue) to the not-so-obvious (your wedding ring) is affected by its environment. Our celebration was held outdoors, and the weather was warm and breezy. On the positive side, my dress's sheer, flowy fabric embraced the breeze. On the "oh shit" side, our table décor was comprised of paper flowers, which had to be weighted with frosted glass. Even on the wedding-band front, the environment of your hands is a key factor to consider. For example, if you build, haul, or construct things with your hands, you may need a more rugged ring (or prongs to ensure gemstones stay put).

Getting back to that venue to-do, my husband and I were ultraconcerned about finding a place that not only met our look and feel requirements, but also had options for families.

STACEY'S ENVIRONMENTAL CONDITIONS

~ Options for friends with kids, and we're pretty kid-friendly
~ Rain backups

 Thinking about your reception venue, list two things that are required by the environment you desire.

YOUR ENVIRONMENTAL CONDITIONS

Note: The workbook will offer environmental influences to consider for each checklist item, so be sure to read the small text to the right of each tab for that extra bit of clarity.

Sample Worksheet

1 IDENTITY STATEMENT

I am • We are • They are a _____ bride • groom • partner • couple (CIRCLE ONE)
(CIRCLE ONE)   ADJECTIVE   wedding party member • helper

and need to find a _____ _____
                              ADJECTIVES   CHECKLIST ITEM

that will feel _____
                              ADJECTIVES, EMOTIONS

and won't _____ or _____ .
              UNWANTED RESULT, FEELING   UNWANTED RESULT

2 ONLINE RESEARCH   Track the websites you've visited and any initial reactions or discoveries.

IHeartThisWebsiteLikeWhoa.com	Notes on why this website kicks ass for our big day

3 STYLE + LOOK   List the ideas, styles, or looks you love. List the things you absolutely despise, too.

LOVE	HATE

4 MaCaW!   What things Must, Could, Won't this to-do have or be? Remember: This is YOUR WEDDING.

MUST	COULD	WON'T

5 ENVIRONMENTAL CONDITIONS   What type of weather, people, travel, etc. does this to-do need to handle?

6 **TIME MACHINE:** FAIL | How will you keep things from going wrong?

This _____ will fail if:

I will avoid this failure by:

7 **TIME MACHINE:** SUCCESS | How will you ensure awesomeness and make everything go right?

This _____ will succeed if:

I will ensure its success by:

8

GET OUT THERE

Prototype Time: GET UP AND TRY THINGS OUT!
Stand in the place you'll say "I do," test-drive those table favors, and imagine you or your guests celebrating. How does it look? Feel? **Make it YOURS — don't settle!**

REMEMBER: THIS IS
YOUR WEDDING!

9 **GET-READY LIST**

Prepare to search and shop or talk with vendors.

BUY / TAKE / ASK / TRY...

10 **VENDOR / IN-STORE RESEARCH**

Who did you visit? What did you learn, decide, discover, love or hate?

VENDORS / PLACES VISITED	NOTES

11 ------- ⊁ LANDING GEAR ENGAGED ⊰ -------

SIZE / QTY / CAPACITY	PRICING NOTES PRICE BREAKS, SHIPPING, ETC.	ORDER / RESERVE-BY SPECIFICS

12 FEELING GOOD ABOUT YOUR DECISION? READY TO ROCK YOUR WEDDING? | CHECK THAT BOX! ❯ ❯❯ ❯❯❯ ☐ **COMPLETE!**

6. TIME MACHINE: FAIL
7. TIME MACHINE: SUCCESS

In the software world, we often run a meeting called a postmortem after a project has been released or reached a certain goal. The key word here is "after." Sometimes it can be too late to change the path ahead for the better. A premortem, however, uses prospective hindsight to get ahead of the troubles and triumphs. We travel forward in time and imagine something has failed in order to plan for the worst- and best-case scenarios. Successes are easy to think of, but fails are frightening! And "postmortem" and "premortem" — yikes! No matter how you slice it, these phrases are pretty macabre. It doesn't feel right to throw a death reference into the beginning of a beautiful life together, does it?

For the AstroWed framework, I've redesigned this kickass planning concept to take on the form of a time machine. As in, hop into this **time machine** and arrive on the day of your wedding. Some things may go better than perfect and others may go terribly wrong. Yes — things going wrong is scary! But any surprise we are ill prepared for will bring on the biggest pile of stress imaginable. As I've mentioned, my husband and I planned on having an entirely outdoor wedding. Guess what? It rained! While we were forced to move the reception inside, we were ready to go with the flow of change thanks to time-machine thinking.

STACEY'S TIME MACHINE: FAIL

This <u>Reception Venue</u> **will fail if:** Everything is à la carte and a million dollars, and we don't have a bad-weather backup.

I will avoid this failure by: Seeing every option these places offer, and asking to see their backup venues.

STACEY'S TIME MACHINE: SUCCESS

This <u>Reception Venue</u> **will succeed if:** Guests find the venue easily, we get the most amazing photos, and everyone has a great time.

I will ensure its success by: Choosing a location that offers something for nearly everyone while trying to make it easy to get to.

 Now you give it a try; **time travel to your wedding day and fill in the blanks below with whatever comes to mind first about your reception venue.**

YOUR TIME MACHINE: FAIL

This <u>Reception Venue</u> **will fail if:**

I will avoid this failure by:

YOUR TIME MACHINE: SUCCESS

This <u>Reception Venue</u> **will succeed if:**

I will ensure its success by:

Note: Keep these things in mind as you begin to chat with vendors before and after booking them.
We made sure to build in time to go around the property to find alternate spaces, should the weather turn for the worst. Our ceremony came with a light sprinkle, and our precious hand-painted paper flowers were moved indoors to an amazing space that had just been renovated. We weren't surprised nor did we morph into 'Zillas. Instead, we may have gone down as the calmest couple in history!

8. PROTOTYPE TIME!

GET UP AND TRY THINGS OUT!

The word *prototype* has a variety of connotations. Some think a prototype must be a tangible thing that costs money and/or time to make. Others think, "Science?! Ugghhh . . ." and run for the hills. I assure you, while this is inspired by a bit of science and a touch of product design, it in no way requires a lab coat or PhD!

Prototyping in AstroWed is usually more about preparing the mind rather than creating something you can hold in your hand (unless of course you're DIYing some crafty goodness). It also serves every wedding item on your checklist. Here's how it works.

- **When you visit a potential ceremony location, stand in the area where you and your partner would say "I do." Does it feel right? Can you envision the photos, and your guests?** THIS is a prototype! You're taking this venue for a test-drive, in essence. Try before you buy, right?

- **The first time you try on a dress, suit, or other awesome wedding outfit,** THIS is a prototype! You're creating a sample of what the to-do *could be.* If it's not right, you try on another, and thus create another prototype experience.

- **If you're creating welcome gift bags for guests and you put a bunch of supplies together to see if your idea will work**, THIS is a prototype! It's a fast but effective method for deciding on the finer details. It's then time to move on to Landing Gear (we'll get to that shortly).

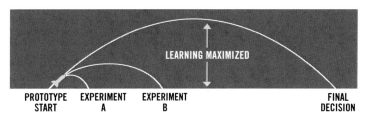

Bottom line: your prototypes will vary. Tangible ones may stem from testing your DIY wedding décor. Larger decisions might come down to imagining your wedding, checking in with your gut to see if it feels right, and then considering other variables like price.

After we fell in love with our venue, we drew up a little paper sketch based on our favorite location on the resort to see if it really would meet all of our needs. Here's how it all came together:

STACEY'S PROTOTYPE NOTES:

Our potential winning venue . . .
- ✔ Is super easy for elderly guests and families with little ones to get to.
- ✔ Has little bits of New England charm, and it'll be like we have part of the resort all to ourselves.
- ✔ Might be too small if we have any more than 70 people.
- ✔ Has rain backups close by.
- ✔ Is laid back with a touch of formality.
- ✔ Dance floor = grassy knoll. Dig it.

**TRY THIS
THOUGHT EXPERIMENT:**

Imagine your guests traveling to and arriving at your venue. Does this picture incorporate everything you listed in the Must column of the **MaCaW** chart? Does it feel like it's part of your wedding universe? If not, what can you change or improve? You may not actually write down loads of notes, but I bet the path forward is clearer, if only because you see what you do or don't like about the options set before you.

HOW TO USE THIS WORKBOOK

9. GET-READY LIST

I'm terrible when it comes to on-the-fly phone calls, interviews, and negotiations. I need to spend a few minutes to prepare the questions, the shopping list, the what to wear, or just the key points necessary for getting the job done. This is the core of the **Get-Ready List**. Use it as your preparatory brain-dumping ground to gear up for that call to the photographer, that DIY favor-shopping trip, or that experience trying on what you might consider to be the most important outfit of your life.

By giving to-dos some proactive forethought, the process of deciding on the biggest parts of the wedding gets easier. Sometimes I'm that anal-retentive overplanner who prepares like it's the end of the world. Other times I don't have an ounce of energy to put towards that stuff. And when I do run out of proactive energy, I ask for help, for someone (or *something* like a fill-in-the-blank worksheet) to do the thinking for me.

I leaned on my wedding party, my closest friends, and my fiancé for certain things because sometimes you just don't have it. THAT'S OKAY! We're human! We have our good days and our bad, and that's exactly why I created AstroWed.

So! This **Get-Ready List** is dedicated to doing the thinking for you, or at the very least, to asking a few questions to get you in get-ready mode. **Take what you've learned in the online research and the questions that have bubbled to the top of your mind and write everything down. Take your notes with you if you're visiting a vendor or store.** For example, if you have a specific undergarment you MUST wear the day of, bring it with you. If you're investigating materials for a special DIY favor or decoration, jot down all possible items you might want to look at, search for, or purchase. And since we've been looking at the reception venue as our primary example . . .

STACEY'S GET-READY LIST

Prepare to find a **Reception Venue** that includes . . .

FIND / ASK / TRY...
Rain alternative locations?
Packaged options vs. à la carte
Flexible on vendors? (we want to bring our own photographer)
Vegetarian/vegan options?
What is included in the wedding package?
How do prices differ on weekdays vs. Friday/Saturday?
Payment schedule?
When is head count needed by?
Rooms: Discounts? Max capacity?
Capacity of venue?
Adult vs. family/kid activities
Any renovations planned on our day?
Standard time of day for weddings?
Rehearsal dinner space?
How many weddings happen in one day normally?

YOUR GET-READY LIST

Prepare to find a **Reception Venue** that includes . . .

FIND / ASK / TRY...

Take this list for a spin. Some of the questions listed at left are fairly standard and may work for you as well, but your wedding might not be outdoors, or you may want to know about things like parking, room style, and so on.

10. VENDOR / IN-STORE RESEARCH

This is the in-person version of the online research. On the DIY side of things, this is where I kept track of things I thought I could buy cheaper elsewhere (Amazon vs. Michaels was always a constant debate!) or needed to go back and look at after trying out an idea.

Here are my high-level notes from our trip to review potential venues:

STACEY'S ON-SITE RESEARCH

What venues or places did you visit? What did you learn, decide, discover, love or hate?

VENUES / PLACES VISITED	NOTES
Postcard Inn	The look of Florida-tchotchke-ville may not sit well with out guests. Once on property, super nice inside hotel and on the grounds. A little too college bro-zone? Also not too much space between multiple wedding locations. Wedding crashers might be a real thing on a Fri/Sat ...
Hawks Cay	Gorgeous drive and quite a beautiful entrance to the property. Signage is clear and the grounds are beautiful. Plenty of options for families and adults, as well as big separation if another wedding is happening while ours is. LOVE THIS PLACE.
Hemingway Home	Never made it. À la carte pricing and cats (allergies) kept us at bay. And we really love Hawks Cay.

If you've visited places already and are in the midst of deciding, filling out this chart should help you see the important aspects right away (and if nothing else, just writing down what's in your head is a quick way to suss out what's best for you and your partner). If you are 100% set, rock and roll! **And, if you have absolutely no clue, you've got questions to take with you on the next wedding-planning journey.**

YOUR ON-SITE RESEARCH

What venues or places did you visit? What did you learn, decide, discover, love or hate?

VENUES / PLACES VISITED	NOTES

11. LANDING GEAR

This is the LAST major section for each wedding to-do! Now it's time to nail down the remaining specifics as you come in for landing with a confident decision:

Size / Quantity / Capacity: How many people do you expect will be present at, will receive, or will use this to-do?

Pricing Notes: How much will this to-do cost? Are there price breaks? Shipping costs? Does it fit into your budget?

Order / Reserve-by Specifics: How many weeks in advance of your wedding day do you need to have this booked, ordered, or shipped by?

Are you ready? Let's do this!

SIZE / QUANTITY / CAPACITY

- ❓ Thinking about table favors? How many guests will be receiving them?
- ❓ Buying special shirts and trousers for the wedding party? List everyone's sizes and write down any tips (i.e., these trousers run small, shrink easily, dry-clean only).
- ❓ Looking at reception venues? How many guests do you envision attending?

Even if you're just getting started, having an estimated count, quantity, or size for most things on the to-do list will help you understand the budgetary differences when asking for a quote, as well as the time an item will take to prep, alter, or have in hand. Sometimes you might need additional details like a maximum and minimum, or note where the price breaks fall to find the best deal. (For example: 50 table favors for $100 vs. 150 for $120.)

STACEY'S CAPACITY + SIZE

Estimated guests: 50
Maximum (est): 70
Minimum (est): 30

Write down your estimated number of seats, your desired maximum, and your desired minimum in the space at right. If you have yet to ask vendors for pricing, use this as a way to understand their capacity for the different rooms or spaces.

If you've already booked your venue, use the number of seats to fuel the fire when it comes to table décor.

YOUR CAPACITY + SIZE

Estimated guests:
Maximum (est):
Minimum (est):

PRICING NOTES

Pretty self-explanatory, right? **For some to-dos it may be as simple as comparing one price to another. For more complex items, you may need to drill down a bit further to really understand the full cost (including shipping and handling, taxes, or reservation fees).** Your reception venue may be all-inclusive, or you may need to ask for the separate prices for the cocktail-hour room and the dining room. And, if you ask these questions up front, there will be less "surprise spending" and therefore less stress!

> **PRO TIP:** When it comes to reception venue pricing, here's a quick list of things to ask about. Items may be included as one or offered separately (this is important to know; ask for both prices):
> - Cocktail-hour room price
> - Dining room price
> - Extras (dance floor, special tables, chair covers, portable toilets, open bar vs. cash bar, planner fee, cake-cutting fee, etc.)

STACEY'S PRICING NOTES

Hawks Cay: $17,000*

*includes ceremony, cocktail hour, and reception with food, bar, and house linens.

 Give your current notes on reception venue pricing in the space below.

YOUR PRICING NOTES

Cocktail-hour Venue: $_____ ____

Cocktail-hour Extras: $_____

Reception Venue: $_____

Reception Extras: $_____

Total Cost: $_____

ORDER / RESERVE-BY SPECIFICS

This section won't apply to every to-do, but it is important to know certain specifics ahead of time so ordering, shipping, and deliveries can be made in time for your big day. For example, it may take up to six months to get your wedding outfit in hand due to customizations or if each piece is made-to-order. Our welcome gifts took about four weeks to arrive at our door, and then we needed time to ship them down to the venue. Scheduling all these moving parts early and often will keep the 'Zillas away.

Did you think the reception venue wouldn't apply here? Guess again!

 If you're in the process of searching for your venue:

YOUR RESEARCH-BY SPECIFICS

> Start researching reception venues by: ____/____
>
> Our reception venue must be booked by: ____/____

 If you've already nailed down your final choice:

YOUR RESERVE-BY SPECIFICS

> Our reception venue must be booked by ___/____
>
> Send venue final head count by ____/____
>
> Send other detail-related choices by ____/____

12. "THIS FEELS F*CKING AMAZING TO CHECK OFF" CHECKBOX

Feeling good about your decision? Ready to rock your wedding? CHECK THAT BOX!

 ☑ COMPLETE!

Grab a marker and soak up the satisfaction! Maybe even celebrate crossing one more thing off with a glass of champagne. You deserve it!

So you've completed your first worksheet, AstroWed style, but what about the rest?

I've got worksheets to support each to-do to help you through your wedding-planning process. And if you're looking for stories, how-tos, and other wedding planning lessons, check out the workbook companion: *Top 10 Wedding Decisions: How to decide without turning into a 'Zilla.*

Fighting off the 'Zillas is hard work. After going through it myself, I get it now! I see how easy it is to get hung up on the wrong details and forget the most important part: **THIS IS YOUR WEDDING!** You can make it yours with less stress and sanity intact.

GET YOUR ROCKET BOOSTERS READY

Holy sh*t, we're engaged. Where and how do we start?

I'm a person who ALWAYS has an answer, a plan, and a backup plan, but when I fell in love with the man who is now my husband and it came time to plan our wedding, I realized that the last time I'd really thought about wedding stuff was when I was a kid. **I was going to get married and name my two children Ariel and Eric because *The Little Mermaid* was the meaning of life.** Fast-forward twenty-six years—I was in need of a serious magic spell.

What the hell did I know about planning a wedding? I had to ask myself, Who is Stacey Dyer? What does she want and not want in a wedding? And what does my partner want?

This is the core of AstroWed: it's a place to learn who you are as individuals and as a couple, then get to the heart of what you're willing to say "I do" and "I don't" to.

So you've said yes. NOW WHAT? There's the initial excitement between the two of you and then come the questions from your friends and family.

Them:
"Congratulations! Have you set a date yet?"
"Where will you have the wedding?"
"What time of year are you thinking about?"

You:
"WE DON'T KNOW YET!"

It's okay to not know. Don't let the well-meaning people in your life stress you out. Planning your own wedding is an overwhelming task, but help is on the way because you're here, reading this book. AstroWed is your ticket to sanity and planning prowess.

So how do we get this wedding-planning party started?

GETTING STARTED

Take a look at the list of to-dos at the right. Even at this early stage, you may see things you couldn't care less about and others you can't imagine doing without. Keep these in mind as we travel to your wedding universe.

👉 **With pen in hand, cross out any to-dos you know aren't relevant in your wedding.** We didn't want a cake or floral arrangements at ours. What are you kicking to the curb?

Then, circle the 10 things you care about the most.

THE MONOLITHIC WEDDING CHECKLIST!

10 – 12 Months Before Your Wedding
- ☐ Budget
- ☐ Guest List, First Pass
- ☐ Ceremony Venue
- ☐ Reception Venue
- ☐ Wedding Planner
- ☐ Officiant
- ☐ Photographer
- ☐ Save-the-Date Announcement

6 – 8 Months Before Your Wedding
- ☐ Color Scheme / Wedding Theme
- ☐ Florist
- ☐ Wedding Party People
- ☐ Attire for Partner No. 1
- ☐ Attire for Partner No. 2
- ☐ Wedding Party Attire, Group 1
- ☐ Wedding Party Attire, Group 2
- ☐ Hairstylist
- ☐ Makeup Artist
- ☐ DJ / Live Band
- ☐ Music Choices
- ☐ Videographer
- ☐ Gift Registry
- ☐ Wedding Website
- ☐ Guest Accommodations
- ☐ Wedding Night Accommodations
- ☐ Transportation

4 – 6 Months Before Your Wedding
- ☐ Ceremony Décor
- ☐ Reception Décor
- ☐ Food + Beverage
- ☐ Cake / Dessert
- ☐ Guest List, Final Version with RSVP Tracker
- ☐ Table Seating Chart
- ☐ Invitations
- ☐ Table Favors
- ☐ Caterer
- ☐ Linens
- ☐ Toast Assignments
- ☐ Ceremony Readings

2 – 3 Months Before Your Wedding
- ☐ Showers-of-Gifts Party
- ☐ Pre-wedding Party for Partner No. 1
- ☐ Pre-wedding Party for Partner No. 2
- ☐ Wedding Rings
- ☐ Honeymoon
- ☐ Welcome Favors
- ☐ Guestbook
- ☐ Custom Vows / Promises
- ☐ Place Cards
- ☐ Photography Shot List
- ☐ Rehearsal (Ceremony)
- ☐ Rehearsal Dinner
- ☐ Marriage License

After Your Wedding
- ☐ Sift through and choose favorite photos
- ☐ Order prints of photos
- ☐ Order / Create a photo album
- ☐ Write thank-you cards

GETTING STARTED

Using the Priority Galaxy on the next page, map out the first cluster of planets in your wedding universe the following way:

- ✔ **Rank your top 10 items from "most important" to "less important," moving left to right.** For example, we cared most about our wedding date, our location, and our photographer. The rest was stuff that needed to get done because it informed other to-dos, like color scheme and wedding party attire.

- ✔ **Write these to-dos in the Priority Galaxy. Most important lives closest to the center (that's YOU!), and the remaining items move to the outer edge.** Be sure to write in your name and your partner's as well. You two are the center of this universe because this is YOUR wedding!

This is not just some funky visual trick; it's a nod to the scientific benefits of writing things down and making decisions. By identifying and prioritizing your top 10 to-dos, you and your awesome partner will make serious progress! Start by tackling the things closest to you, the most meaningful things, and you'll feel like superheroes when they're completed.

> **PRO TIP:** As you move further out into the galaxy, the smaller size of the to-do planets should remind you that they're not as important. **If these items start stressing you out, just take another look at what's most meaningful to you both. Regroup, then knock it out of the park with a "good enough for now" approach.**

When you reviewed that checklist the first time, how did you feel? Now that you've filled out the Priority Galaxy, how do you feel?

> **PRO TIP: Your pen is mightier than your mother-in-law's opinion.** Neutralize stress by writing down what matters to you two.

There will be plenty of other details to address beyond your top 10, but consider this your first step towards stress-free planning. Furthermore, I encourage you to make copies of the Priority Galaxy (or head to Astro-Wed.com for more!) to help you divide and conquer other clusters of to-dos. Getting stuff out of your head and onto paper is a decision, and decisions equal happiness. You're getting married to the person you love! Keep the happiness factor in focus.

PRIORITY GALAXY

Identify your top 10 wedding to-dos, then map out your star system below.

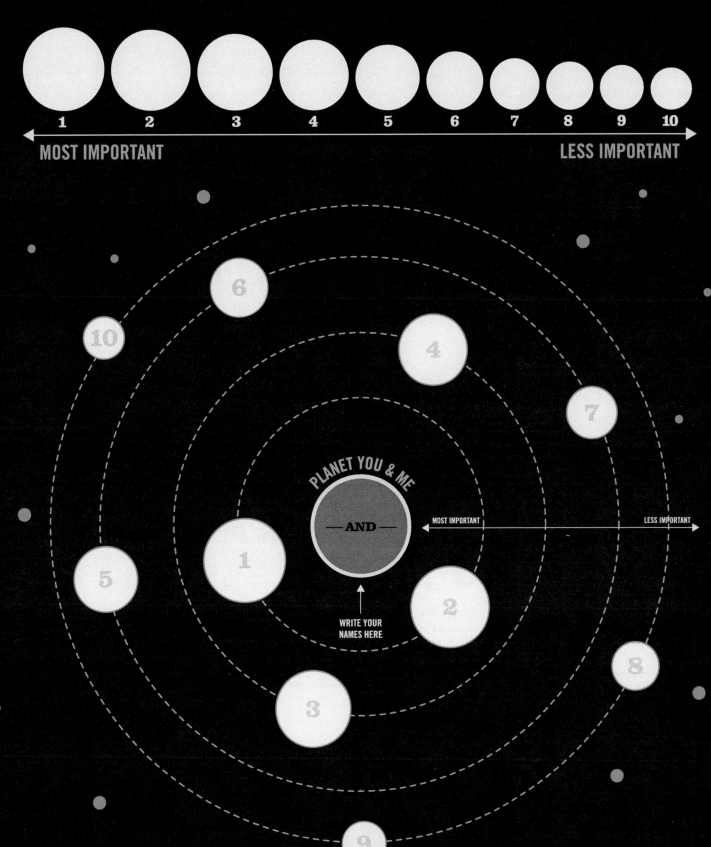

GETTING STARTED

Okay! Using your Priority Galaxy and the contents list before each section (like on page 37), locate the worksheet for <u>Planet Number 1</u>. Get started with what is most important to you.

Note that the workbook has been organized into sections based on suggested wedding timelines; however, I encourage you to break the mold and start with what's most important to you. Remember, this is YOUR WEDDING and YOUR UNIVERSE!

And now a message from our sponsors . . .

'Zilla(s) *zih•lə(z)*
noun

An alien-induced neurological condition that primarily occurs when a human undergoes extreme stress due to wedding planning, especially when focused on too many unprioritized details or microdecisions swimming around in one's head, rendering all means of communication dangerous or nonexistent or both.

How to Fight Off 'Zillas
Write down what you know, love, and hate. Write down what you don't know, your fears, your concerns. Inhale. Exhale. Your now-healthy mental state transfers to the breath, creating exhalations of stability and balance. 'Zillas will find this type of breath to be like fire and run far, far away.

NOTE: AstroWeddicists highly recommend the use of the AstroWed Workbook to aid in such processes.

Start fighting off 'Zillas, today! Use the Priority Galaxy or begin with the page at right.

THINGS TO CONSIDER
10 – 12 MONTHS
BEFORE YOUR WEDDING

1 WE CAN SPEND...

Personal money: _____

Money from other sources: _____

Total Money We Can Spend:
$_____

2 ESTIMATED BUDGET CALCULATOR

WEDDING EXPENSE	% OF BUDGET	YOU MAY SPEND . . .
Ceremony & Reception (venues, food and beverage, tips, etc.)	50%	
Attire for You and Your Partner (dress, suit, tailoring, accessories)	10%	
Décor (Floral or Otherwise) (ceremony, reception decorations, floral, etc.)	10%	
Photography / Video (shooting of your wedding, prints, etc.)	12%	
Music / Entertainment (bands, DJs, instrumental musicians, etc.)	10%	
Favors & Gifts (table and welcome favors, wedding party gifts)	3%	
Invitations & Other Paper Stuff (place cards, programs, signage, table favors)	2%	
Transportation (limos, Lambos, Royces, F-150s)	1%	
Wedding Rings (for you and your partner)	2%	
Total	100%	

3

After you've taken a look at your **Estimated Budget** (all percentages are based on industry data), use the **Priority + Reality Budget Calculator** to determine what matters most to the two of you. **For example:** we spent about 20% on our photography and 1% on our invitations.

Here's the two-step process:

1. **Using the "Priority" column below, rank the wedding expenses below on a scale of 1 to 9** (1 being the most important and 9 being the least).

2. **Assign a percentage to each expense, based on your priority ranking.** Or, if that's fuzzy, assign dollar amounts first — what you know you'd be willing to spend on music, for example. Then divide what you will spend by the total budget and voila! There's your percentage (For example: **$2500 on music / $25,000 total money = 0.10 or 10%**)

That's it!

Now you've got a wedding budget that's based on what matters to the both of you and your wallets, rather than the wedding industry.

#thismathrocks

4 PRIORITY + REALITY BUDGET CALCULATOR

WEDDING EXPENSE	PRIORITY	% OF BUDGET	YOU WILL SPEND . . .
Ceremony & Reception (venues, food and beverage, tips, etc.)			
Attire for You and Your Partner (dress, suit, tailoring, accessories)			
Décor (Floral or Otherwise) (ceremony, reception decorations, floral, etc.)			
Photography / Video (shooting of your wedding, prints, etc.)			
Music / Entertainment (bands, DJs, instrumental musicians, etc.)			
Favors & Gifts (table and welcome favors, wedding party gifts)			
Invitations & Other Paper Stuff (place cards, programs, signage, table favors)			
Transportation (limos, Lambos, Royces, F-150s)			
Wedding Rings (for you and your partner)			
Total			

5 FEELING GOOD ABOUT YOUR BUDGET? READY TO ROCK YOUR WEDDING?

CHECK THAT BOX! ❯❯❯ ▢ COMPLETE!

Guest List, First Pass

GUEST LIST, FINAL VERSION + RSVP IS ON **PAGE 91**

1 IDENTITY STATEMENT

I am • We are • They are a _____ bride • groom • partner • couple (CIRCLE ONE)
(CIRCLE ONE)   ADJECTIVE   wedding party member • helper

and need to invite _____ **Guests.**
                        ADJECTIVES   CHECKLIST ITEM

2 MaCaW! What couples and individuals _Must_, _Could_, _Won't_ be on this Guest List? Remember: This is YOUR WEDDING.

MUST INVITE		COULD INVITE
1) Ariel & Sebastian	35)	70)
2)	36)	71)
3)	37)	72)
4)	38)	73)
5)	39)	74)
6)	40)	75)
7)	41)	76)
8)	42)	77)
9)	43)	78)
10)	44)	79)
11)	45)	80)
12)	46)	81)
13)	47)	82)
14)	48)	83)
15)	49)	84)
16)	50)	85)
17)	51)	86)
18)	52)	87)
19)	53)	88)
20)	54)	89)
21)	55)	90)
22)	56)	

WON'T INVITE
No.
Nope.
No way.
Never.
Not them.
Or them.
Hell no.
Over my dead body.

23)	57)
24)	58)
25)	59)
26)	60)
27)	61)
28)	62)
29)	63)
30)	64)
31)	65)
32)	66)
33)	67)
34)	68)
	69)

Estimated No. of Guests: [ ]

3 FEELING GOOD ABOUT YOUR **FIRST PASS AT A GUEST LIST?** READY TO ROCK YOUR WEDDING?

CHECK THAT BOX! ≫ ≫ ≫ [ ] **COMPLETE!**

FIND VENUE BY: ___/___　GUESTS: _____　BUDGET: $_____

Cermony Venue

1 IDENTITY STATEMENT

I am • We are • They are a _____ bride • groom • partner • couple (CIRCLE ONE)
　(CIRCLE ONE)　　　　　　　ADJECTIVE　　　　wedding party member • helper

and need to find a _____ __Ceremony Venue__
　　　　　　　　　　　　　　ADJECTIVES　　　　　　　　　CHECKLIST ITEM

that will feel _____
　　　　　　　　　　　　　　　　　ADJECTIVES, EMOTIONS

and won't _____ or _____.
　　　　UNWANTED RESULT, FEELING　　　　　　　　UNWANTED RESULT

2 ONLINE RESEARCH   Track the websites you've visited and any initial reactions or discoveries.

IHeartThisWebsiteLikeWhoa.com	Notes on why this venue kicks ass for our big day

3 STYLE + LOOK   List the __Ceremony__ styles or looks you __love__. List the things you __absolutely despise__, too.

LOVE	HATE

4 MaCaW!   What _Must, Could, Won't_ this __Ceremony Venue__ have or be? Remember: This is YOUR WEDDING.

MUST	COULD	WON'T

5 ENVIRONMENTAL CONDITIONS   What type of weather, capacity, or guests does your __Ceremony Venue__ need to handle?

6 **TIME MACHINE:** FAIL   How will you keep things from going wrong?

This **Ceremony Venue** will fail if:

I will avoid this failure by:

7 **TIME MACHINE:** SUCCESS   How will you ensure awesomeness and make everything go right?

This **Ceremony Venue** will succeed if:

I will ensure its success by:

---

8   GET OUT THERE   **Check out real ceremonies on-site,** stand in the place you'll say "I do," and imagine your guests there. How does the ceremony venue feel? Look?

REMEMBER: THIS IS
YOUR WEDDING!

9 **GET-READY LIST**

Prepare to search and shop, or talk with vendors.

BUY / TAKE / ASK / TRY. . .

10 **IN-PERSON CEREMONY VENUE RESEARCH**

Who did you visit? What did you learn, decide, discover, love or hate?

VENDORS / PLACES VISITED	NOTES

11 -----))) LANDING GEAR ENGAGED (((-----

CAPACITY + SIZE

PRICING NOTES   WEEKEND VS. WEEKDAY, ETC.

RESERVE-VENUE-BY SPECIFICS

12 FEELING GOOD ABOUT YOUR **CEREMONY VENUE**?
READY TO ROCK YOUR WEDDING?   CHECK THAT BOX! ⟩⟩⟩   ☐ COMPLETE!

FIND VENUE BY: ___/___   GUESTS: _____   BUDGET: $_____

1 IDENTITY STATEMENT

I am • We are • They are a _____ bride • groom • partner • couple (CIRCLE ONE)
(CIRCLE ONE)   ADJECTIVE   wedding party member • helper

and need to find a _____ **Reception Venue**
                                    ADJECTIVES   CHECKLIST ITEM

that will feel _____
                                        ADJECTIVES, EMOTIONS

and won't _____ or _____.
              UNWANTED RESULT, FEELING   UNWANTED RESULT

2 ONLINE RESEARCH   Track the websites you've visited and any initial reactions or discoveries.

IHeartThisWebsiteLikeWhoa.com	Notes on why this venue kicks ass for our big day

3 STYLE + LOOK   List the Reception styles or looks you love. List the things you absolutely despise, too.

LOVE	HATE

4 MaCaW!   What *Must, Could, Won't* this Reception Venue have or be? Remember: This is YOUR WEDDING.

MUST	COULD	WON'T

5 ENVIRONMENTAL CONDITIONS   What type of weather, capacity, or guests does your Reception Venue need to handle?

6 TIME MACHINE: FAIL   How will you keep things from going wrong?

This **Reception Venue** will fail if:

I will avoid this failure by:

7 TIME MACHINE: SUCCESS   How will you ensure awesomeness and make everything go right?

This **Reception Venue** will succeed if:

I will ensure its success by:

8

GET OUT THERE

Secretly crash a wedding at the site (with the help of the on-site coordinator), try the food, and imagine celebrating with your guests at this reception venue. How does it look? Feel?

REMEMBER: THIS IS
YOUR WEDDING!

9 GET-READY LIST

Prepare to search and shop, or talk with vendors.

BUY / TAKE / ASK / TRY...

10 IN-PERSON RECEPTION VENUE RESEARCH

Who did you visit? What did you learn, decide, discover, love or hate?

VENDORS / PLACES VISITED	NOTES

11   ✈))) LANDING GEAR ENGAGED (((✈

CAPACITY + SIZE	PRICING NOTES WEEKEND VS. WEEKDAY, ETC.	RESERVE-VENUE-BY SPECIFICS

12
FEELING GOOD ABOUT YOUR **RECEPTION VENUE?**
READY TO ROCK YOUR WEDDING?   CHECK THAT BOX! ⟩ ⟩ ⟩   ☐ COMPLETE!

FIND VENDOR BY: ___/___   GUESTS: _____   BUDGET: $_____

1 IDENTITY STATEMENT

I am • We are • They are a _____   bride • groom • partner • couple   (CIRCLE ONE)
(CIRCLE ONE)   ADJECTIVE   wedding party member • helper

and need to find a _____   <u>Wedding Planner</u>
                                            ADJECTIVES   CHECKLIST ITEM

who will feel _____
                                            ADJECTIVES, EMOTIONS

and won't _____ or _____.
              UNWANTED RESULT, FEELING   UNWANTED RESULT

2 ONLINE RESEARCH   Track the websites you've visited and any initial reactions or discoveries.

IHeartThisWebsiteLikeWhoa.com	Notes on why this planner kicks ass for our big day

3 STYLE + LOOK   List the <u>Planning</u> styles or approaches you <u>love</u>. List the things you <u>absolutely despise</u>, too.

LOVE	HATE

4 MaCaW!   What *Must, Could, Won't* this <u>Wedding Planner</u> do or provide? Remember: This is YOUR WEDDING.

MUST	COULD	WON'T

5 ENVIRONMENTAL CONDITIONS   What type of weather, activities, or guests does your <u>Wedding Planner</u> need to handle?

6 **TIME MACHINE:** FAIL   How will you keep things from going wrong?

This **Wedding Planner** will fail if:

I will avoid this failure by:

7 **TIME MACHINE:** SUCCESS   How will you ensure awesomeness and make everything go right?

This **Wedding Planner** will succeed if:

I will ensure his/her success by:

8   GET OUT THERE   **Pick up that phone and talk to people.**
What are the different approaches? Email back and
forth a bit with wedding planners. Do they fit your
communication needs?

REMEMBER: THIS IS
YOUR WEDDING!

9 **GET-READY LIST**
Prepare to search and shop, or talk with vendors.

BUY / TAKE / ASK / TRY. . .

10 **IN-PERSON WEDDING PLANNER RESEARCH**
Who did you visit? What did you learn, decide, discover, love or hate?

VENDORS / PLACES VISITED	NOTES

11 - - - - - - - - - - - - - - - ⟨ LANDING GEAR ENGAGED ⟩ - - - - - - - - - -

SERVICES OFFERED	PRICING NOTES	TO-DO LIST FOR HER / HIM

12 FEELING GOOD ABOUT YOUR **WEDDING PLANNER**?
READY TO ROCK YOUR WEDDING?   CHECK THAT BOX! ⟩⟩ ⟩⟩⟩   ☐ COMPLETE!

FIND VENDOR BY: ___/___   GUESTS: _____   BUDGET: $_____

1 IDENTITY STATEMENT

I am • We are • They are a _____ bride • groom • partner • couple (CIRCLE ONE)
(CIRCLE ONE)   ADJECTIVE   wedding party member • helper

and need to find an _____ **Officiant**
                              ADJECTIVES   CHECKLIST ITEM

who will feel _____
                              ADJECTIVES, EMOTIONS

and won't _____ or _____.
          UNWANTED RESULT, FEELING   UNWANTED RESULT

2 ONLINE RESEARCH   Track the websites you've visited and any initial reactions or discoveries.

IHeartThisWebsiteLikeWhoa.com	Notes on why this officiant kicks ass for our big day

3 STYLE + LOOK   List the Officiating styles or looks you love. List the things you absolutely despise, too.

LOVE	HATE

4 MaCaW!   What Must, Could, Won't your Officiant do or provide? Remember: This is YOUR WEDDING.

MUST	COULD	WON'T

5 ENVIRONMENTAL CONDITIONS   What weather, special guests, or special ceremonies does your Officiant need to handle?

6 TIME MACHINE: FAIL — How will you keep things from going wrong?

Our **Officiant** will fail if:

I will avoid this failure by:

7 TIME MACHINE: SUCCESS — How will you ensure awesomeness and make everything go right?

Our **Officiant** will succeed if:

I will ensure his/her success by:

8

GET OUT THERE

Ask for samples of readings and for the format of other weddings he or she has officiated. How would you change things to make it more "you two"? Does the officiant truly "get" you?

REMEMBER: THIS IS
YOUR WEDDING!

9 GET-READY LIST
Prepare to search and shop, or talk with vendors.

BUY / TAKE / ASK / TRY. . .

10 IN-PERSON OFFICIANT RESEARCH
Who did you visit? What did you learn, decide, discover, love or hate?

VENDORS / PLACES VISITED	NOTES

11 ◀))) LANDING GEAR ENGAGED (((✈

SERVICES OFFERED

PRICING NOTES

TIMELINE SPECIFICS

12 FEELING GOOD ABOUT YOUR **OFFICIANT**? READY TO ROCK YOUR WEDDING?

CHECK THAT BOX! 〉〉〉 〉〉〉 ☐ COMPLETE!

Photographer

FIND VENDOR BY: ___/___ GUESTS: _____ BUDGET: $_____

1 IDENTITY STATEMENT

I am • We are • They are a _____ bride • groom • partner • couple (CIRCLE ONE)
(CIRCLE ONE)   ADJECTIVE   wedding party member • helper

and need to find a _____ **Photographer**
                                    ADJECTIVES   CHECKLIST ITEM

who will feel _____
                                    ADJECTIVES, EMOTIONS

and won't _____ or _____ .
            UNWANTED RESULT, FEELING   UNWANTED RESULT

2 ONLINE RESEARCH — Track the websites you've visited and any initial reactions or discoveries.

IHeartThisWebsiteLikeWhoa.com	Notes on why this photographer kicks ass for our big day

3 STYLE + LOOK — List the Photography styles or looks you love. List the things you absolutely despise, too.

LOVE	HATE

4 MaCaW! — What Must, Could, Won't your Photographer do or provide? Remember: This is YOUR WEDDING.

MUST	COULD	WON'T

5 ENVIRONMENTAL CONDITIONS — What weather, venue, or lighting does your Photographer need to handle?

6 TIME MACHINE: FAIL   How will you keep things from going wrong?

Our **Photographer** will fail if:

I will avoid this failure by:

7 TIME MACHINE: SUCCESS   How will you ensure awesomeness and make everything go right?

Our **Photographer** will succeed if:

I will ensure his/her success by:

8

GET OUT THERE → Look through the portfolios of your top three photographers and imagine you and your partner in those shots. **Can you see these images representing your love for all time?**

REMEMBER: THIS IS
YOUR WEDDING!

9 GET-READY LIST
Prepare to search and shop, or talk with vendors.

BUY / TAKE / ASK / TRY . . .

10 IN-PERSON PHOTOGRAPHER RESEARCH
Who did you visit? What did you learn, decide, discover, love or hate?

VENDORS / PLACES VISITED	NOTES

11 ------ 《》 LANDING GEAR ENGAGED 《》 ------

PACKAGES OFFERED	PRICING NOTES	CONTRACTUAL SPECIFICS

12 FEELING GOOD ABOUT YOUR **PHOTOGRAPHER**? READY TO ROCK YOUR WEDDING?   CHECK THAT BOX! ➤➤➤ ☐ COMPLETE!

Save-the-Date

1 IDENTITY STATEMENT

I am • We are • They are a _____ bride • groom • partner • couple (CIRCLE ONE)
(CIRCLE ONE)   ADJECTIVE   wedding party member • helper

and need to find a _____ Save-the-Date Announcement
                                                    ADJECTIVES   CHECKLIST ITEM

that will feel _____
                                                    ADJECTIVES, EMOTIONS

and won't _____ or _____.
                    UNWANTED RESULT, FEELING   UNWANTED RESULT

2 ONLINE RESEARCH   Track the websites you've visited and any initial reactions or discoveries.

IHeartThisWebsiteLikeWhoa.com	Notes on why this website kicks ass for our big day

3 STYLE + LOOK   List the Save-the-Date Announcement styles or looks you love. List the things you absolutely despise, too.

LOVE	HATE

4 MaCaW!   What Must, Could, Won't this Save-the-Date Announcement have or be? Remember: This is YOUR WEDDING.

MUST	COULD	WON'T

5 ENVIRONMENTAL CONDITIONS   What type of weather, capacity, or guests does your Save-the-Date need to handle/include?

6 TIME MACHINE: FAIL How will you keep things from going wrong?

This **Save-the-Date** will fail if:

I will avoid this failure by:

7 TIME MACHINE: SUCCESS How will you ensure awesomeness and make everything go right?

This **Save-the-Date** will succeed if:

I will ensure its success by:

8 GET OUT THERE

Grab some paper and sketch out how you'd like your announcement to look — even if you're not a designer! Just blocking things out can help you realize your save-the-date.

REMEMBER: THIS IS
YOUR WEDDING!

9 STUFF YOU NEED TO SAY

What do you want to say on this Save-the-Date?

CONSIDER INCLUDING...

Wedding date

Location (town or specific place)

Your names

"Details (invitation, etc.) to follow" message

Colors?

Photo(s) you'd like to use?

10 DRAW YOUR IDEAS HERE

11 SKETCH EVEN MORE SAVE-THE-DATE IDEAS HERE

12 ·········· 〉〉〉 LANDING GEAR ENGAGED 〈〈〈 ··········

QUANTITY + PRICING NOTES

PRICE BREAKS, SHIPPING, ETC.

IF YOU'RE PRINTING THESE SAVE-THE-DATES…	PRICING NOTES
Single-sided or Double-sided?	
Full Color or Black & White?	
Fancy Print Accents? (foils, etc.)	
Envelopes? (number of / cost of)	
Stamps? (number of / cost of)	

ORDER / MAKE THINGS BY…

13 FEELING GOOD ABOUT YOUR **SAVE-THE-DATE**? READY TO ROCK YOUR WEDDING? CHECK THAT BOX! 〉〉〉 ☐ COMPLETE!

THINGS TO CONSIDER
6 – 8 MONTHS
BEFORE YOUR WEDDING

Other to-dos that might pertain to you at this stage:

- Videographer
- Gift registry
- Wedding-night accommodations (for you two)
- Transportation (fancy or practical)
- Guest accommodations
- Wedding website

Keep Your To-Dos Happy

with a trip on the AstroWed Time Machine

NEED TO DECIDE BY: ___/___   GUESTS: _____   BUDGET: $_____

Wedding Theme

1 IDENTITY STATEMENT

I am • We are • They are a _____ bride • groom • partner • couple (CIRCLE ONE)
  (CIRCLE ONE)   ADJECTIVE   wedding party member • helper

  and need to find a _____ __Wedding Theme__
                                          ADJECTIVES   CHECKLIST ITEM

  that will feel _____
                                          ADJECTIVES, EMOTIONS

  and won't _____ or _____ .
                  UNWANTED RESULT, FEELING   UNWANTED RESULT

2 ONLINE RESEARCH   Track the websites you've visited and any initial reactions or discoveries.

IHeartThisWebsiteLikeWhoa.com	Notes on why this website kicks ass for our big day

3 STYLE + LOOK   List the __Wedding Theme__ styles or looks you __love__. List the things you __absolutely despise__, too.

LOVE	HATE

4 MaCaW!   What _Must_, _Could_, _Won't_ this __Wedding Theme__ have or be? Remember: This is YOUR WEDDING.

MUST	COULD	WON'T

5 ENVIRONMENTAL CONDITIONS   What type of climate, capacity, or guests does your __Wedding Theme__ need to handle?

6 TIME MACHINE: FAIL   How will you keep things from going wrong?

This **Wedding Theme** will fail if:

I will avoid this failure by:

7 TIME MACHINE: SUCCESS   How will you ensure awesomeness and make everything go right?

This **Wedding Theme** will succeed if:

I will ensure its success by:

8

GET OUT THERE

Make a brainstorm board on Pinterest, get analog and cut out ideas from magazines and catalogs, buy and try a couple of centerpiece ideas, or talk to a few vendors about your wedding theme.

REMEMBER: THIS IS
YOUR WEDDING!

9 GET-READY LIST
Prepare to search and shop, or talk with vendors.

BUY / TAKE / ASK / TRY. . .

10 IN-PERSON WEDDING THEME RESEARCH
Who did you visit? What did you learn, decide, discover, love or hate?

VENDORS / PLACES VISITED	NOTES

11 - - - - - - - - - - - - - - - LANDING GEAR ENGAGED - - - - - - - - - - - - - -

QUANTITY / CAPACITY	PRICING NOTES PRICE BREAKS, SHIPPING, ETC.	ORDER / MAKE THINGS BY...

12 FEELING GOOD ABOUT YOUR **WEDDING THEME**? READY TO ROCK YOUR WEDDING?   CHECK THAT BOX! ≫≫≫   ☐ COMPLETE!

Color Scheme Laboratory

(1) **Tape, paste, or draw ideas here,** then when you've narrowed things down to your final choice, create your master color palette below. *(For more on how to use this color palette technique, check out Astro-Wed.com.)*

(2) MASTER PALETTE

Wedding color palettes are often made of the following five-part formula:

1. A bold color
2. A secondary accent color to complement "big bold" up there
3. A light or dark base (the background, the tablecloths, etc.)
4. Neutral #1 (think about natural elements in centerpieces, colors your parents might wear)
5. Neutral #2 (to round out the color family)

CUT & GLUE STRIPS OF COLOR TO CREATE YOUR MASTER PALETTE

1   2   3   4   5

(3) **Create smaller groups of color by applying the Master Palette to other elements such as table favors, wedding party outfits, and centerpieces.**
Using markers, crayons, scraps of paper pulled from magazines, or paper samples, try laying out some of the palettes for your bigger elements. *(For examples and other info, check out Astro-Wed.com.)*

PALETTE FOR _____'S OUTFIT

RECEPTION DÉCOR PALETTE

PALETTE FOR _____'S OUTFIT

CEREMONY DÉCOR PALETTE

WEDDING-PARTY MEMBERS PALETTE (GROUP 1)

INVITATION PALETTE

WEDDING-PARTY MEMBERS PALETTE (GROUP 2)

FAVORS PALETTE

OUTFIT PALETTE FOR PARENTS OF _____

PALETTE FOR _____

OUTFIT PALETTE FOR PARENTS OF _____

PALETTE FOR _____

(4) FEELING GOOD ABOUT YOUR **COLOR SCHEME?** READY TO ROCK YOUR WEDDING? CHECK THAT BOX! ▷ ▷▷ ▷▷▷ ☐ COMPLETE!

60

FIND VENDOR BY: ___/___ **GUESTS:** _____ **BUDGET: $**_____

Florist

1 IDENTITY STATEMENT

I am • We are • They are a _____
(CIRCLE ONE)   ADJECTIVE

bride • groom • partner • couple (CIRCLE ONE)
wedding party member • helper

and need to find a _____ __**Florist**__
                                    ADJECTIVES   CHECKLIST ITEM

who will feel _____
                              ADJECTIVES, EMOTIONS

and won't _____ or _____.
                UNWANTED RESULT, FEELING   UNWANTED RESULT

2 ONLINE RESEARCH
Track the websites you've visited and any initial reactions or discoveries.

IHeartThisWebsiteLikeWhoa.com	Notes on why this website kicks ass for our big day

3 STYLE + LOOK
List the __Floral__ styles or looks you __love__. List the things you __absolutely despise__, too.

LOVE	HATE

4 MaCaW!
What *Must*, *Could*, *Won't* this __Florist__ have or be? Remember: This is YOUR WEDDING.

MUST	COULD	WON'T

5 ENVIRONMENTAL CONDITIONS
What type of weather or guests (kids vs. adults) does your __Florist__ need to handle?

6 TIME MACHINE: FAIL   How will you keep things from going wrong?

This **Florist** will fail if:

I will avoid this failure by:

7 TIME MACHINE: SUCCESS   How will you ensure awesomeness and make everything go right?

This **Florist** will succeed if:

I will ensure his/her success by:

8

GET OUT THERE

After narrowing down your choices to two or three florists, ask if they can create or show you arrangement samples that meet your design needs. Or create your own to bring as an example.

REMEMBER: THIS IS
YOUR WEDDING!

9 GET-READY LIST

Prepare to search and shop, or talk with vendors.

BUY / TAKE / ASK / TRY. . .

10 IN-PERSON FLORIST RESEARCH

Who did you visit? What did you learn, decide, discover, love or hate?

VENDORS / PLACES VISITED	NOTES

11 ------------------- ✈ LANDING GEAR ENGAGED ✈ -------------------

QUANTITY / SIZE

PRICING NOTES

ORDER SPECIFICS

12 FEELING GOOD ABOUT YOUR **FLORIST**?
READY TO ROCK YOUR WEDDING?   **CHECK THAT BOX!** ❯ ❯ ❯ ❯   ☐ **COMPLETE!**

Wedding Party People

1 IDENTITY STATEMENT

I am • We are • They are a _____ bride • groom • partner • couple (CIRCLE ONE)
(CIRCLE ONE)   ADJECTIVE   wedding party member • helper

and need to find _____ <u>Wedding Party People</u>
                            ADJECTIVES   CHECKLIST ITEM

who will feel _____
                              ADJECTIVES, EMOTIONS

and won't _____ or _____ .
              UNWANTED RESULT, FEELING   UNWANTED RESULT

2 MaCaW! Who *Must, Could, Won't* be in your <u>Wedding Party</u>? Remember: This is YOUR WEDDING.

MUST	COULD	WON'T

3 ROLES + APPROACHES TO THIS WEDDING PARTY PEOPLE THING

TRADITIONAL ROUTE	NON-TRADITIONAL ROUTE	SUPERHERO HELPERS
Bridesmaids	Bridesmate	Task Master
Matron / Maid of Honor	Matron / Maid of Alcohol, Sanity, Love	DIY Crafter
Groomsmen	Man of Honor	Emergency Nurse
Best Man	Lady of Distinction	Party Starter
Flower Girl / Boy	Gentleman of Distinction	Music Master

4 WHO'S WHO

NAME	THIS PERSON'S ROLE	NAME	THIS PERSON'S ROLE

63

Other Roles for Wedding Party People and Wedding Helpers

✦ Trusted advisor on major decisions

✦ Design helper for décor, accessories, and more

✦ Organizer of the bridal shower

✦ Organizer of the bachelorette party

✦ Hands-on DIY crafter

✦ Bridal party outfit tester

✦ Accessory decision-maker

✦ Handmade item triage nurse (for when something breaks)

✦ Angel of tiny details (place cards, accents on favors, etc.)

✦ Baker of delectable goods (for the masses or just in general — food is life!)

✦ Task master for making sure the other wedding party has their shit together

✦ Phone tree manager when times or locations of key events change

✦ Emergency nurse, i.e., keeper of all bandages and pain-relief remedies

✦ Motivational music master

✦ Filler of cups — libations or other forms of hydration

✦ Bouquet holder

✦ Entertainer of ring bearers

✦ Introducer of this guest to that guest

✦ Sanity checker

Attire for:

NEED TO DECIDE BY: ___/___ BUDGET: $_____

1 IDENTITY STATEMENT

I am • We are • They are a _____ bride • groom • partner • couple (CIRCLE ONE)
(CIRCLE ONE)   ADJECTIVE   wedding party member • helper

and need to find _____ **Attire (Dress, Suit, Outfit)**
                                    ADJECTIVES   CHECKLIST ITEM

that will feel _____
                                    ADJECTIVES, EMOTIONS

and won't _____ or _____.
                    UNWANTED RESULT, FEELING   UNWANTED RESULT

2 ONLINE RESEARCH   Track the websites you've visited and any initial reactions or discoveries.

IHeartThisWebsiteLikeWhoa.com	Notes on why this website kicks ass for the big day

3 STYLE + LOOK   List the Attire styles or looks you love. List the things you absolutely despise, too.

LOVE	HATE

4 MaCaW!   What Must, Could, Won't your Attire do or be? Remember: This is YOUR WEDDING.

MUST	COULD	WON'T

5 ENVIRONMENTAL CONDITIONS   What weather, dancing, or events does your Attire need to handle?

6 TIME MACHINE: FAIL   How will you keep things from going wrong?

My **Attire** will fail if:

I will avoid this failure by:

7 TIME MACHINE: SUCCESS   How will you ensure awesomeness and make everything go right?

My **Attire** will succeed if:

I will ensure its success by:

8 GET OUT THERE   **Hit up a few shops, take some risks** and try on lots of different styles, and take accessories similar to what you think you'll wear on the big day. How does your attire make you feel?

REMEMBER: THIS IS
YOUR WEDDING!

9 GET-READY LIST
Prepare to search and shop, or talk with vendors.

BUY / TAKE / ASK / TRY . . .

10 IN-PERSON ATTIRE RESEARCH
Who did you visit? What did you learn, decide, discover, love or hate?

VENDORS / PLACES VISITED	NOTES

11 ----- ✈ LANDING GEAR ENGAGED ✈ -----

SIZE + TAILORING NOTES	PRICING NOTES	ORDER + PICKUP SPECIFICS

12 FEELING GOOD ABOUT YOUR **ATTIRE**?
READY TO ROCK YOUR WEDDING?   CHECK THAT BOX! ❯ ❯ ❯❯❯ ☐ COMPLETE!

NEED TO DECIDE BY: ___/___ BUDGET: $_____

Attire for:

1 IDENTITY STATEMENT

I am • We are • They are a _____ bride • groom • partner • couple (CIRCLE ONE)
(CIRCLE ONE)   ADJECTIVE   wedding party member • helper

and need to find _____ Attire (Dress, Suit, Outfit)
                              ADJECTIVES   CHECKLIST ITEM

that will feel _____
                              ADJECTIVES, EMOTIONS

and won't _____ or _____.
                UNWANTED RESULT, FEELING   UNWANTED RESULT

2 ONLINE RESEARCH   Track the websites you've visited and any initial reactions or discoveries.

IHeartThisWebsiteLikeWhoa.com	Notes on why this website kicks ass for the big day

3 STYLE + LOOK   List the Attire styles or looks you love. List the things you absolutely despise, too.

LOVE	HATE

4 MaCaW!   What Must, Could, Won't your Attire do or be? Remember: This is YOUR WEDDING.

MUST	COULD	WON'T

5 ENVIRONMENTAL CONDITIONS   What weather, dancing, or events does your Attire need to handle?

6 **TIME MACHINE:** FAIL   How will you keep things from going wrong?

My **Attire** will fail if:

I will avoid this failure by:

7 **TIME MACHINE:** SUCCESS   How will you ensure awesomeness and make everything go right?

My **Attire** will succeed if:

I will ensure its success by:

8 GET OUT THERE

Hit up a few shops, take some risks and try on lots of different styles, and take accessories similar to what you think you'll wear on the big day. How does your attire make you feel?

REMEMBER: THIS IS
YOUR WEDDING!

9 **GET-READY LIST**
Prepare to search and shop, or talk with vendors.

BUY / TAKE / ASK / TRY...

10 **IN-PERSON ATTIRE RESEARCH**
Who did you visit? What did you learn, decide, discover, love or hate?

VENDORS / PLACES VISITED	NOTES

11 ▸))) LANDING GEAR ENGAGED ((◂

SIZE + TAILORING NOTES	PRICING NOTES	ORDER + PICKUP SPECIFICS

12 FEELING GOOD ABOUT YOUR **ATTIRE**?
READY TO ROCK YOUR WEDDING?   CHECK THAT BOX! ❯ ❯ ❯ ❯   ☐ COMPLETE!

Wedding Party Attire:

1 IDENTITY STATEMENT

I am • We are • They are a _____ bride • groom • partner • couple (CIRCLE ONE)
(CIRCLE ONE)   ADJECTIVE   wedding party member • helper

and need to find _____ **Wedding Party Attire, Group 1**
                                         ADJECTIVES   CHECKLIST ITEM

that will feel _____
                                              ADJECTIVES, EMOTIONS

and won't _____ or _____.
                  UNWANTED RESULT, FEELING   UNWANTED RESULT

2 ONLINE RESEARCH   Track the websites you've visited and any initial reactions or discoveries.

IHeartThisWebsiteLikeWhoa.com	Notes on why this website kicks ass for the big day

3 STYLE + LOOK   List the Wedding Party Attire styles or looks you love. List the things you absolutely despise, too.

LOVE	HATE

4 MaCaW!   What Must, Could, Won't your Wedding Party's Attire do or be? Remember: This is YOUR WEDDING.

MUST	COULD	WON'T

5 ENVIRONMENTAL CONDITIONS   What weather, dancing, or events does your Wedding Party's Attire need to handle?

6 TIME MACHINE: FAIL   How will you keep things from going wrong?

Group 1's Attire will fail if:

I will avoid this failure by:

7 TIME MACHINE: SUCCESS   How will you ensure awesomeness and make everything go right?

Group 1's Attire will succeed if:

I will ensure its success by:

---

8 GET OUT THERE

Order some stuff. Try on some stuff.
Return the stuff that doesn't work.
Imagine your wedding party in your future photos.
How does Group 1's attire look?

REMEMBER: THIS IS
YOUR WEDDING!

---

9 GET-READY LIST

Prepare to search and shop, or talk with vendors.

BUY / TAKE / ASK / TRY...

10 IN-PERSON WEDDING PARTY ATTIRE RESEARCH

Who did you visit, order from? What did you learn, decide, discover, love or hate?

VENDORS / PLACES VISITED	NOTES

---

11 - - - - - - - - - - - - - - - - - -))) LANDING GEAR ENGAGED (((- - - - - - - - - - - - -

SIZE + TAILORING NOTES	PRICING NOTES	ORDER + PICKUP SPECIFICS

---

12 FEELING GOOD ABOUT **GROUP 1'S ATTIRE?**
READY TO ROCK YOUR WEDDING?   CHECK THAT BOX! 〉〉 〉〉〉   ☐ COMPLETE!

Wedding Party Attire:

1 IDENTITY STATEMENT

I am • We are • They are a _____   bride • groom • partner • couple   (CIRCLE ONE)
(CIRCLE ONE)   ADJECTIVE   wedding party member • helper

and need to find _____ **Wedding Party Attire, Group 2**
                         ADJECTIVES   CHECKLIST ITEM

that will feel _____
                         ADJECTIVES, EMOTIONS

and won't _____ or _____ .
         UNWANTED RESULT, FEELING   UNWANTED RESULT

2 ONLINE RESEARCH
Track the websites you've visited and any initial reactions or discoveries.

IHeartThisWebsiteLikeWhoa.com	Notes on why this website kicks ass for the big day

3 STYLE + LOOK
List the <u>Wedding Party Attire</u> styles or looks you <u>love</u>. List the things you <u>absolutely despise</u>, too.

LOVE	HATE

4 MaCaW!
What *Must, Could, Won't* your <u>Wedding Party's Attire</u> do or be? Remember: This is YOUR WEDDING.

MUST	COULD	WON'T

5 ENVIRONMENTAL CONDITIONS
What weather, dancing, or events does your <u>Wedding Party's Attire</u> need to handle?

6 **TIME MACHINE:** FAIL — How will you keep things from going wrong?

Group 2's Attire will fail if:

I will avoid this failure by:

7 **TIME MACHINE:** SUCCESS — How will you ensure awesomeness and make everything go right?

Group 2's Attire will succeed if:

I will ensure its success by:

8 GET OUT THERE

Order some stuff. Try on some stuff. Return the stuff that doesn't work. Imagine your wedding party in your future photos. How does **Group 2's attire** look?

REMEMBER: THIS IS

YOUR WEDDING!

9 **GET-READY LIST**

Prepare to search and shop, or talk with vendors.

BUY / TAKE / ASK / TRY...

10 **IN-PERSON WEDDING PARTY ATTIRE RESEARCH**

Who did you visit, order from? What did you learn, decide, discover, love or hate?

VENDORS / PLACES VISITED	NOTES

11 - - - - - - - LANDING GEAR ENGAGED - - - - - - -

SIZE + TAILORING NOTES	PRICING NOTES	ORDER + PICKUP SPECIFICS

12 FEELING GOOD ABOUT **GROUP 2'S ATTIRE?** READY TO ROCK YOUR WEDDING?   CHECK THAT BOX! ≫ ≫ ≫ ☐ COMPLETE!

FIND VENDOR BY: ___/___   NO. OF PEOPLE TO BE STYLED: _____   BUDGET:_____

1 IDENTITY STATEMENT

I am • We are • They are a _____   bride • groom • partner • couple (CIRCLE ONE)
(CIRCLE ONE)   ADJECTIVE   wedding party member • helper

and need to find a _____   **Hairstylist**
                                                    ADJECTIVES   CHECKLIST ITEM

who will feel _____
                                                        ADJECTIVES, EMOTIONS

and won't _____ or _____.
                    UNWANTED RESULT, FEELING   UNWANTED RESULT

2 ONLINE RESEARCH   Track the websites you've visited and any initial reactions or discoveries.

IHeartThisWebsiteLikeWhoa.com	Notes on terminology, hairstyles, things to ask/look for

3 STYLE + LOOK   List the Hairstyles or looks you love. List the things you absolutely despise, too.

LOVE	HATE

4 MaCaW!   What Must, Could, Won't your Hairstylist do or provide? Remember: This is YOUR WEDDING.

MUST	COULD	WON'T

5 ENVIRONMENTAL CONDITIONS   What type of weather, specialty accents, dye, or cut does your Hairstylist need to handle?

6 TIME MACHINE: FAIL How will you keep things from going wrong?

This **Hairstylist** will fail if:

I will avoid this failure by:

7 TIME MACHINE: SUCCESS How will you ensure awesomeness and make everything go right?

This **Hairstylist** will succeed if:

I will ensure his/her success by:

8 **GET OUT THERE** **Research hairstyles until you have a few that feel like BFFs.** Talk to your current hairstylist about how possible things are/are not. Talk to a couple of vendors. Get a trial run!

REMEMBER: THIS IS YOUR WEDDING!

9 GET-READY LIST
Prepare to search and shop, or talk with vendors.

BUY / TAKE / ASK / TRY. . .

10 IN-PERSON HAIRSTYLIST RESEARCH
Who did you visit? What did you learn, decide, discover, love or hate?

VENDORS / PLACES VISITED	NOTES

11 - - - - - - - - - - - - - - - - LANDING GEAR ENGAGED - - - - - - - - - -

SERVICES OFFERED	PRICING NOTES	TIMELINE SPECIFICS

12 FEELING GOOD ABOUT YOUR **HAIRSTYLIST**?
READY TO ROCK YOUR WEDDING? CHECK THAT BOX! ▶ ▶ ▶ ☐ **COMPLETE!**

Makeup Artist

1 IDENTITY STATEMENT

I am • We are • They are a _____ bride • groom • partner • couple (CIRCLE ONE)
(CIRCLE ONE)   ADJECTIVE   wedding party member • helper

and need to find a _____ **Makeup Artist**
                                    ADJECTIVES   CHECKLIST ITEM

who will feel _____
                                        ADJECTIVES, EMOTIONS

and won't _____ or _____ .
                UNWANTED RESULT, FEELING   UNWANTED RESULT

2 ONLINE RESEARCH   Track the websites you've visited and any initial reactions or discoveries.

IHeartThisWebsiteLikeWhoa.com	Notes on terminology, makeup colors, tones, things to ask/look for

3 STYLE + LOOK   List the Makeup styles or looks you love. List the things you absolutely despise, too.

LOVE	HATE

4 MaCaW!   What Must, Could, Won't your Makeup Artist do or provide? Remember: This is YOUR WEDDING.

MUST	COULD	WON'T

5 ENVIRONMENTAL CONDITIONS   What type of weather and skin type does your Makeup Artist need to handle?

6 TIME MACHINE: FAIL   How will you keep things from going wrong?

This **Makeup Artist** will fail if:

I will avoid this failure by:

7 TIME MACHINE: SUCCESS   How will you ensure awesomeness and make everything go right?

This **Makeup Artist** will succeed if:

I will ensure his/her success by:

8 GET OUT THERE

Watch tutorials.
Stare at magazines.
Pinterest like crazy.

Head to the mall and get a makeover to test-drive what you think will be good for your makeup artist to know.

REMEMBER: THIS IS YOUR WEDDING!

9 GET-READY LIST

Prepare to search and shop, or talk with vendors.

BUY / TAKE / ASK / TRY. . .

10 IN-PERSON MAKEUP ARTIST RESEARCH

Who did you visit? What did you learn, decide, discover, love or hate?

VENDORS / PLACES VISITED	NOTES

11))) LANDING GEAR ENGAGED (((

SERVICES OFFERED	PRICING NOTES	TIMELINE SPECIFICS

12 FEELING GOOD ABOUT YOUR **MAKEUP ARTIST?** READY TO ROCK YOUR WEDDING?   CHECK THAT BOX! > > >> ☐ COMPLETE!

FIND VENDOR BY: ___/___   GUESTS: _____   BUDGET: $_____

DJ / Live Band

1 IDENTITY STATEMENT

I am • We are • They are a _____ bride • groom • partner • couple (CIRCLE ONE)
(CIRCLE ONE)   ADJECTIVE   wedding party member • helper

and need to find a _____ **DJ / Live Band**
                              ADJECTIVES   CHECKLIST ITEM

that will feel _____
                              ADJECTIVES, EMOTIONS

and won't _____ or _____ .
            UNWANTED RESULT, FEELING   UNWANTED RESULT

2 ONLINE RESEARCH   Track the websites you've visited and any initial reactions or discoveries.

IHeartThisWebsiteLikeWhoa.com	Notes on why this website kicks ass for our big day

3 STYLE + LOOK   List the styles of music you love. List the stuff you absolutely despise, too.

LOVE	HATE

4 MaCaW!   What Must, Could, Won't your DJ / Live Band do or provide? Remember: This is YOUR WEDDING.

MUST	COULD	WON'T

5 ENVIRONMENTAL CONDITIONS   What types of guests or special requests does your DJ / Live Band need to handle?

77

6 TIME MACHINE: FAIL — How will you keep things from going wrong?

Our **DJ / Live Band** will fail if:

I will avoid this failure by:

7 TIME MACHINE: SUCCESS — How will you ensure awesomeness and make everything go right?

Our **DJ / Live Band** will succeed if:

I will ensure their success by:

---

8 GET OUT THERE

Watch video footage of your top three DJs or Live Bands. Check out their song lists. Are they open to special requests? Will they answer to the crowd's desires or yours?

REMEMBER: THIS IS YOUR WEDDING!

9 GET-READY LIST
Prepare to search and shop, or talk with vendors.

BUY / TAKE / ASK / TRY...

10 IN-PERSON DJ / LIVE BAND RESEARCH
Who did you visit? What did you learn, decide, discover, love or hate?

VENDORS / PLACES VISITED	NOTES

11))) LANDING GEAR ENGAGED (((

SERVICES OFFERED	PRICING NOTES	TIMELINE SPECIFICS

12 FEELING GOOD ABOUT YOUR **DJ / LIVE BAND?** READY TO ROCK YOUR WEDDING? **CHECK THAT BOX!** ☐ **COMPLETE!**

NEED TO SEND TO DJ / LIVE BAND BY: ___/___

① MUSICAL ARCHITECTURE OF A WEDDING

CEREMONY MUSIC	MUSIC THAT PLAYS AS . . .	WE WANT	HELL NO
Ceremony Prelude Music	Guests arrive and get seated for the ceremony		
1st Ceremony Processional Song	Parents and/or the first group of wedding party members file in		
2nd Ceremony Processional Song	Partner No. 2 and/or the second group of wedding party members file in		
3rd Ceremony Processional Song	Partner No. 1 walks down the aisle		
Recessional Song	You leave the ceremony. You're married! Celebrate like crazy!		
RECEPTION: INTRODUCTION MUSIC	**MUSIC THAT PLAYS AS . . .**		
Parents of Partner No. 1 Song	Parents of Partner No. 1 are announced		
Parents of Partner No. 2 Song	Parents of Partner No. 2 are announced		
Wedding Party Group 1 Song	Group 1 wedding party members are announced		
Wedding Party Group 2 Song	Group 2 wedding party members are announced		
Newlywed Couple Intro Song	You two are introduced for the first time as a married couple!!!		
RECEPTION: SPECIAL DANCES	**WHAT HAPPENS DURING THIS DANCE?**		
First Dance Song	Your first dance as a married couple (YAY!)		
Parent/Partner No. 1 Dance Song	Partner No. 1 dances with special parent		
Parent/Partner No. 2 Dance Song	Partner No. 2 dances with special parent		
Cake-cutting Song	Let them eat cake! (And shove it in each other's faces)		
Bouquet-toss Song	Who's gonna be the lucky person to catch that bouquet?		
Garter-removal Song	Tradition's bit of risqué theater		
Garter-toss Song	Who's gonna be the lucky person to catch that garter?		

GET OUT THERE

Now that you know the different parts that could have specific music, **list the songs that are top of mind, right now.** Use the **MaCaW** chart to help prototype and organize your ideas.

② MaCaW! What *Must, Could, Won't* your Music or Songs include? Remember: This is YOUR WEDDING.

MUST	COULD	WON'T

3 CEREMONY MUSIC

CEREMONY PART	SONG / MUSIC GENRE	ARTIST

4 RECEPTION: INTRODUCTION MUSIC

INTRODUCING...	SONG / MUSIC GENRE	ARTIST

5 RECEPTION: SPECIAL DANCES

DANCE / EVENT	SONG / MUSIC GENRE	ARTIST

6 RECEPTION: DANCE PARTY

THESE SONGS MUST GET PLAYED	THESE TOO	DO NOT PLAY THESE SONGS OR ELSE...

7 FEELING GOOD ABOUT YOUR MUSIC CHOICES? READY TO ROCK YOUR WEDDING? CHECK THAT BOX! ▶▶▶ ☐ COMPLETE!

Other to-dos that might pertain to you at this stage:
- Caterer
- Linens
- Toast assignments
- Ceremony readings

NEED TO DECIDE BY: ___/___   GUESTS: _____   BUDGET: $_____

Ceremony Décor

1 IDENTITY STATEMENT

I am • We are • They are a _____ bride • groom • partner • couple (CIRCLE ONE)
                          (CIRCLE ONE)   ADJECTIVE   wedding party member • helper

and need to find _____ Ceremony Décor
                                    ADJECTIVES   CHECKLIST ITEM

that will feel _____
                                    ADJECTIVES, EMOTIONS

and won't _____ or _____.
              UNWANTED RESULT, FEELING   UNWANTED RESUIT

2 ONLINE RESEARCH   Track the websites you've visited and any initial reactions or discoveries.

IHeartThisWebsiteLikeWhoa.com	Notes on why this website kicks ass for our big day

3 STYLE + LOOK   List the Ceremony Décor styles or looks you love. List the things you absolutely despise, too.

LOVE	HATE

4 MaCaW!   What Must, Could, Won't this Ceremony Décor have or be? Remember: This is YOUR WEDDING.

MUST	COULD	WON'T

5 ENVIRONMENTAL CONDITIONS   What type of weather, capacity, or guests does your Ceremony Décor need to handle?

6 TIME MACHINE: FAIL
How will you keep things from going wrong?

This **Ceremony Décor** will fail if:

I will avoid this failure by:

7 TIME MACHINE: SUCCESS
How will you ensure awesomeness and make everything go right?

This **Ceremony Décor** will succeed if:

I will ensure its success by:

8

GET OUT THERE

Take photos of your ceremony venue and cut and paste, digitally apply, or simply imagine your décor ideas there. How do these ideas look? Do they suit you two?

REMEMBER: THIS IS
YOUR WEDDING!

9 GET-READY LIST
Prepare to search and shop, or talk with vendors.

BUY / TAKE / ASK / TRY...

10 IN-PERSON CEREMONY DÉCOR RESEARCH
Who did you visit? What did you learn, decide, discover, love or hate?

VENDORS / PLACES VISITED	NOTES

11
))) LANDING GEAR ENGAGED (((

QUANTITY + SIZE

PRICING NOTES

ORDER / MAKE THINGS BY...

12
FEELING GOOD ABOUT YOUR **CEREMONY DÉCOR**? READY TO ROCK YOUR WEDDING?

CHECK THAT BOX! ▷ ▷ ▷ ☐ **COMPLETE!**

NEED TO DECIDE BY: ___/___   GUESTS: _____   BUDGET: $_____

Reception Décor

1 IDENTITY STATEMENT

I am • We are • They are a _____ bride • groom • partner • couple (CIRCLE ONE)
(CIRCLE ONE)   ADJECTIVE   wedding party member • helper

and need to find _____ **Reception Décor**
                              ADJECTIVES   CHECKLIST ITEM

that will feel _____
                              ADJECTIVES, EMOTIONS

and won't _____ or _____.
              UNWANTED RESULT, FEELING   UNWANTED RESULT

2 ONLINE RESEARCH   Track the websites you've visited and any initial reactions or discoveries.

IHeartThisWebsiteLikeWhoa.com	Notes on why this website kicks ass for our big day

3 STYLE + LOOK   List the Reception Décor styles or looks you love. List the things you absolutely despise, too.

LOVE	HATE

4 MaCaW!   What Must, Could, Won't this Reception Décor have or be? Remember: This is YOUR WEDDING.

MUST	COULD	WON'T

5 ENVIRONMENTAL CONDITIONS   What type of weather, capacity, or guests does your Reception Décor need to handle?

6 TIME MACHINE: FAIL How will you keep things from going wrong?

This **Reception Décor** will fail if:

I will avoid this failure by:

7 TIME MACHINE: SUCCESS How will you ensure awesomeness and make everything go right?

This **Reception Décor** will succeed if:

I will ensure its success by:

8

GET OUT THERE

Sketch your reception décor ideas on paper and look at photos of other weddings held at your venue. Imagine being there with your partner-to-be. Can you see the celebration?

REMEMBER: THIS IS
YOUR WEDDING!

9 GET-READY LIST
Prepare to search and shop, or talk with vendors.

BUY / TAKE / ASK / TRY . . .

10 IN-PERSON RECEPTION DÉCOR RESEARCH
Who did you visit? What did you learn, decide, discover, love or hate?

VENDORS / PLACES VISITED	NOTES

11 — — — — — LANDING GEAR ENGAGED — — — — —

CAPACITY + SIZE	PRICING NOTES	ORDER / MAKE THINGS BY...

12 FEELING GOOD ABOUT YOUR **RECEPTION DÉCOR?**
READY TO ROCK YOUR WEDDING? **CHECK THAT BOX!** ⟩⟩⟩ ☐ **COMPLETE!**

NEED TO DECIDE BY: ___/___   GUESTS: _____   BUDGET: $_____

Food + Beverage

1 IDENTITY STATEMENT

I am • We are • They are a _____ bride • groom • partner • couple (CIRCLE ONE)
(CIRCLE ONE)   ADJECTIVE   wedding party member • helper

and need to find _____ **Food + Beverage**
                              ADJECTIVES   CHECKLIST ITEM

that will feel _____
                              ADJECTIVES, EMOTIONS

and won't _____ or _____.
              UNWANTED RESULT, FEELING   UNWANTED RESULT

2 ONLINE RESEARCH   Track the websites you've visited and any initial reactions or discoveries.

IHeartThisWebsiteLikeWhoa.com	Notes on why this website kicks ass for our big day

3 STYLE + LOOK   List the Food + Beverage styles or looks you love. List the things you absolutely despise, too.

LOVE	HATE

4 MaCaW!   What Must, Could, Won't this Food + Beverage have or be? Remember: This is YOUR WEDDING.

MUST	COULD	WON'T

5 ENVIRONMENTAL CONDITIONS   What weather or guests (kids, adults, vegans, etc.) does your Food + Beverage need to handle?

6 TIME MACHINE: FAIL   How will you keep things from going wrong?

This **Food + Beverage** will fail if:

I will avoid this failure by:

7 TIME MACHINE: SUCCESS   How will you ensure awesomeness and make everything go right?

This **Food + Beverage** will succeed if:

I will ensure its success by:

8

GET OUT THERE

Enjoy MANY tastings and perhaps cheers with a custom cocktail! Does the food and beverage meet your guests' preferences? Is there stuff you two love as well?

REMEMBER: THIS IS
YOUR WEDDING!

9 GET-READY LIST

Prepare to search and shop, or talk with vendors.

BUY / TAKE / ASK / TRY . . .

10 IN-PERSON FOOD + BEVERAGE RESEARCH

What did you taste or try? What did you learn, decide, discover, love or hate?

VENDORS / PLACES VISITED	NOTES

11 - 🚀))) L A N D I N G   G E A R   E N G A G E D (((🚀 - - - - - - - - - - - - - - - - - - -

QUANTITY / CAPACITY	PRICING NOTES	RESERVE / ORDER-BY SPECIFICS

12 FEELING GOOD ABOUT YOUR FOOD + BEVERAGE? READY TO ROCK YOUR WEDDING?   CHECK THAT BOX! ≫≫≫   ☐ COMPLETE!

FIND VENDOR BY: ___/___   GUESTS: _____   BUDGET: $_____

Cake / Dessert

1 IDENTITY STATEMENT

I am • We are • They are a _____ bride • groom • partner • couple (CIRCLE ONE)
(CIRCLE ONE)   ADJECTIVE   wedding party member • helper

and need to find a _____ **Cake / Dessert**
                                ADJECTIVES   CHECKLIST ITEM

that will feel _____
                                        ADJECTIVES, EMOTIONS

and won't _____ or _____.
              UNWANTED RESULT, FEELING   UNWANTED RESULT

2 ONLINE RESEARCH   Track the websites you've visited and any initial reactions or discoveries.

IHeartThisWebsiteLikeWhoa.com	Notes on why this website kicks ass for our big day

3 STYLE + LOOK   List the Cake / Dessert styles or looks you love. List the things you absolutely despise, too.

LOVE	HATE

4 MaCaW!   What Must, Could, Won't this Cake / Dessert have or be? Remember: This is YOUR WEDDING.

MUST	COULD	WON'T

5 ENVIRONMENTAL CONDITIONS   What weather or guests (gluten-free, vegans, etc.) does your Cake / Dessert need to handle?

6 TIME MACHINE: FAIL   How will you keep things from going wrong?

This **Cake / Dessert** will fail if:

I will avoid this failure by:

7 TIME MACHINE: SUCCESS   How will you ensure awesomeness and make everything go right?

This **Cake / Dessert** will succeed if:

I will ensure its success by:

8

GET OUT THERE

Indulge and eat cake! Or cupcakes!
Or Turkish delights! Whatever your cake or dessert,
does it meet your guests' needs? Does it meet yours?

REMEMBER: THIS IS
YOUR WEDDING!

9 GET-READY LIST

Prepare to search and shop, or talk with vendors.

BUY / TAKE / ASK / TRY. . .

10 IN-PERSON CAKE / DESSERT RESEARCH

Who did you visit? What did you learn, decide, discover, love or hate?

VENDORS / PLACES VISITED	NOTES

11 ✈))) LANDING GEAR ENGAGED (((✈

QUANTITY / CAPACITY	PRICING NOTES	ORDER-BY SPECIFICS

12 FEELING GOOD ABOUT YOUR **CAKE / DESSERT**? READY TO ROCK YOUR WEDDING?   CHECK THAT BOX! ▷▷▷ ☐ COMPLETE!

NEED ALL GUEST RESPONSES BY: ___/___

NOTE: Couples count as TWO GUESTS. 40 couples = 80 guests

COUPLE / INDIVIDUAL NAMES	ADDRESS	RSVP: YES	RSVP: NO	FOOD PREF
1) Luke & Buzz				
2)				
3)				
4)				
5)				
6)				
7)				
8)				
9)				
10)				
11)				
12)				
13)				
14)				
15)				
16)				
17)				
18)				
19)				
20)				
21)				
22)				
23)				
24)				
25)				
26)				
27)				
28)				
29)				
30)				
31)				
32)				
33)				
34)				
35)				
36)				
37)				
38)				
39)				
40)				
41)				
42)				
43)				
44)				
45)				

COUPLE / INDIVIDUAL NAMES	ADDRESS	RSVP: YES	RSVP: NO	FOOD PREF
46)				
47)				
47)				
48)				
49)				
50)				
51)				
52)				
53)				
54)				
55)				
56)				
57)				
58)				
59)				
60)				
61)				
62)				
63)				
64)				
65)				
66)				
67)				
68)				
69)				
70)				
71)				
72)				
73)				
74)				
75)				
76)				
77)				
78)				
79)				
80)				
81)				
82)				
83)				
84)				
85)				
86)				
87)				
88)				
89)				
90)				
91)				
92)				
93)				

COUPLE / INDIVIDUAL NAMES	ADDRESS	RSVP: YES	RSVP: NO	FOOD PREF
94)				
95)				
96)				
97)				
98)				
99)				
100)				
101)				
102)				
103)				
104)				
105)				
106)				
107)				
108)				
109)				
110)				
111)				
112)				
113)				
114)				
115)				
116)				
117)				
118)				
119)				
120)				
121)				
122)				
123)				
124)				
125)				
126)				
127)				
128)				
129)				
130)				
131)				
132)				
133)				
134)				
135)				
136)				
137)				
138)				
139)				
140)				
141)				
142)				

COUPLE / INDIVIDUAL NAMES	ADDRESS	RSVP: YES	RSVP: NO	FOOD PREF
143)				
144)				
145)				
146)				
147)				
148)				
149)				
150)				
151)				
152)				
153)				
154)				
155)				
156)				
157)				
158)				
159)				
160)				
161)				
162)				
163)				
163)				
164)				
165)				
166)				
167)				
168)				
169)				
170)				
171)				
172)				
173)				
174)				
175)				
176)				
177)				
178)				
179)				
180)				

FEELING GOOD ABOUT YOUR **GUEST LIST + RSVP**s?
READY TO ROCK YOUR WEDDING?   CHECK THAT BOX! 〉〉〉〉〉〉 ☐ COMPLETE!

NEED TO CREATE BY: ___/___
NEED TO SEND BY: ___/___   GUESTS: _____   BUDGET: $_____

Invitations

1 IDENTITY STATEMENT

I am • We are • They are a _____ bride • groom • partner • couple (CIRCLE ONE)
(CIRCLE ONE)   ADJECTIVE   wedding party member • helper

and need to find _____ **Invitations**
                        ADJECTIVES   CHECKLIST ITEM

that will feel _____
                            ADJECTIVES, EMOTIONS

and won't _____ or _____.
          UNWANTED RESULT, FEELING   UNWANTED RESULT

2 ONLINE RESEARCH   Track the websites you've visited and any initial reactions or discoveries.

IHeartThisWebsiteLikeWhoa.com	Notes on why this website kicks ass for our big day

3 STYLE + LOOK   List the Invitation styles or looks you love. List the things you absolutely despise, too.

LOVE	HATE

4 MaCaW!   What Must, Could, Won't your Invitations have or be? Remember: This is YOUR WEDDING.

MUST	COULD	WON'T

5 ENVIRONMENTAL CONDITIONS   What type of readers, language, or travel do your Invitations need to handle?

6 **TIME MACHINE:** FAIL   How will you keep things from going wrong?

Our **Invitations** will fail if:
....

I will avoid this failure by:
....

7 **TIME MACHINE:** SUCCESS   How will you ensure awesomeness and make everything go right?

Our **Invitations** will succeed if:
....

I will ensure their success by:
....

8

GET OUT THERE

Draw a few ideas, outline all of the stuff you want to say, or hop to cool paper stores to look at samples. Also, make sure your elderly guests will be able to read these invitations as well as the young'uns.

REMEMBER: THIS IS
YOUR WEDDING!

9 **STUFF THAT COULD BE SAID**

What do you want to say on your invitations?

CONSIDER INCLUDING...

Your Names

Parents' Names (Mr. & Mrs. Smith request your attendance at the marriage of their...)

Wedding Date, Day of the Week

Wedding Logo

Ceremony Location

Ceremony Time

Reception Location

Reception Time

RSVP by This Date

Wedding Website

Gift Registry Store(s) or Website(s)

A Little Story about You Two

Accommodations for Guests

RSVP Card and Envelope (or website link)

Main Envelope

10 **DRAW YOUR IDEAS HERE**

11 SKETCH EVEN MORE INVITATION IDEAS HERE

12 - ◀))) LANDING GEAR ENGAGED (((▶ - - - - - - - - - - - - - - - - - - -

QUANTITY + PRICING NOTES

PRICE BREAKS, SHIPPING, ETC.

ORDER / MAKE THINGS BY...

IF YOU'RE PRINTING THESE SAVE-THE-DATES...	PRICING NOTES
Main invitation cards	
Ancillary info cards (map, accommodations, etc.)	
RSVP cards	
RSVP envelopes	
Outer/main envelopes	
Stamps? (number of stamps, total cost)	

13 FEELING GOOD ABOUT YOUR **INVITATIONS**?
READY TO ROCK YOUR WEDDING?   CHECK THAT BOX! ›› ››› ☐ COMPLETE!

Seating Chart: Tables 1 – 8

NEED TO SEND TO VENUE BY: ___/___

① **TABLE 1**

NAMES (INDIVIDUALS AND COUPLES)

TABLE 5

NAMES (INDIVIDUALS AND COUPLES)

TABLE 2

NAMES (INDIVIDUALS AND COUPLES)

TABLE 6

NAMES (INDIVIDUALS AND COUPLES)

TABLE 3

NAMES (INDIVIDUALS AND COUPLES)

TABLE 7

NAMES (INDIVIDUALS AND COUPLES)

TABLE 4

NAMES (INDIVIDUALS AND COUPLES)

TABLE 8

NAMES (INDIVIDUALS AND COUPLES)

Seating Chart: Tables 9 – 16

TABLE 9

NAMES (INDIVIDUALS AND COUPLES)

TABLE 13

NAMES (INDIVIDUALS AND COUPLES)

TABLE 10

NAMES (INDIVIDUALS AND COUPLES)

TABLE 14

NAMES (INDIVIDUALS AND COUPLES)

TABLE 11

NAMES (INDIVIDUALS AND COUPLES)

TABLE 15

NAMES (INDIVIDUALS AND COUPLES)

TABLE 12

NAMES (INDIVIDUALS AND COUPLES)

TABLE 16

NAMES (INDIVIDUALS AND COUPLES)

Seating Chart: Tables 17 – 24

TABLE 17
NAMES (INDIVIDUALS AND COUPLES)

TABLE 21
NAMES (INDIVIDUALS AND COUPLES)

TABLE 18
NAMES (INDIVIDUALS AND COUPLES)

TABLE 22
NAMES (INDIVIDUALS AND COUPLES)

TABLE 19
NAMES (INDIVIDUALS AND COUPLES)

TABLE 23
NAMES (INDIVIDUALS AND COUPLES)

TABLE 20
NAMES (INDIVIDUALS AND COUPLES)

TABLE 24
NAMES (INDIVIDUALS AND COUPLES)

2 FEELING GOOD ABOUT YOUR **SEATING CHART?**
READY TO ROCK YOUR WEDDING? **CHECK THAT BOX!** >>> ☐ COMPLETE!

NEED TO DECIDE BY: ___/___   GUESTS: _____   BUDGET: $_____

Table Favors

1 IDENTITY STATEMENT

I am • We are • They are a _____ bride • groom • partner • couple (CIRCLE ONE)
(CIRCLE ONE)   ADJECTIVE   wedding party member • helper

and need to find _____ **Table Favors**
                            ADJECTIVES   CHECKLIST ITEM

that will feel _____
                                        ADJECTIVES, EMOTIONS

and won't _____ or _____ .
                UNWANTED RESULT, FEELING   UNWANTED RESULT

2 ONLINE RESEARCH   Track the websites you've visited and any initial reactions or discoveries.

IHeartThisWebsiteLikeWhoa.com	Notes on why this website kicks ass for our big day

3 STYLE + LOOK   List the Table Favor styles or looks you love. List the things you absolutely despise, too.

LOVE	HATE

4 MaCaW!   What Must, Could, Won't your Table Favors do or provide? Remember: This is YOUR WEDDING.

MUST	COULD	WON'T

5 ENVIRONMENTAL CONDITIONS   What type of weather and travel do your Table Favors need to handle?

6 TIME MACHINE: FAIL   How will you keep things from going wrong?

These **Table Favors** will fail if:

I will avoid this failure by:

7 TIME MACHINE: SUCCESS   How will you ensure awesomeness and make everything go right?

These **Table Favors** will succeed if:

I will ensure their success by:

8

GET OUT THERE

Purchase some samples, create a sample place setting, and have your friends, helpers, or wedding party members weigh in on the experience of these "Thank you for coming" table favors.

REMEMBER: THIS IS
YOUR WEDDING!

9 GET-READY LIST

Prepare to search and shop, or talk with vendors.

BUY / TAKE / ASK / TRY . . .

10 IN-PERSON TABLE FAVORS RESEARCH

Who did you visit? What did you learn, decide, discover, love or hate?

VENDORS / PLACES VISITED	NOTES

11))) LANDING GEAR ENGAGED (((

QUANTITY / SIZE	PRICING NOTES	ORDERING SPECIFICS

12 FEELING GOOD ABOUT YOUR **TABLE FAVORS?** READY TO ROCK YOUR WEDDING?   CHECK THAT BOX! ›› ›› ››   ☐ COMPLETE!

THINGS TO CONSIDER
2 – 3 MONTHS
BEFORE YOUR WEDDING

Other to-dos that might pertain to you at this stage:
- Welcome favors
- Guestbook
- Custom vows/promises
- Place cards
- Photography shot list
- Rehearsal (ceremony)
- Rehearsal dinner
- Marriage license

PLAN PARTY BY: ___/___

GUESTS: _____   BUDGET: $_____

Showers-of-Gifts Party*

Think bridal showers, anti-showers, Jack & Jills, etc.

1 IDENTITY STATEMENT

I am • We are • They are a _____ bride • groom • partner • couple (CIRCLE ONE)
(CIRCLE ONE)   ADJECTIVE   wedding party member • helper

and need a _____ Showers-of-Gifts Party
                        ADJECTIVES   CHECKLIST ITEM

that will feel _____
                              ADJECTIVES, EMOTIONS

and won't _____ or _____ .
          UNWANTED RESULT, FEELING   UNWANTED RESULT

2 ONLINE RESEARCH   Track the websites you've visited and any initial reactions or discoveries.

IHeartThisWebsiteLikeWhoa.com	Notes on why this website kicks ass for our big day

3 STYLE + LOOK   List the Showers-of-Gifts Party styles and looks you love. List the things you absolutely despise, too.

LOVE	HATE

4 MaCaW!   What *Must, Could, Won't* your Showers-of-Gifts Party do or provide? Remember: This is YOUR WEDDING.

MUST	COULD	WON'T

5 ENVIRONMENTAL CONDITIONS   What type of weather or attendees does your Showers-of-Gifts Party need to handle?

6 TIME MACHINE: FAIL How will you keep things from going wrong?

This **Showers-of-Gifts Party** will fail if:

I will avoid this failure by:

7 TIME MACHINE: SUCCESS How will you ensure awesomeness and make everything go right?

This **Showers-of-Gifts Party** will succeed if:

I will ensure its success by:

8

GET OUT THERE

If you're planning this shower for yourself, use this area to jot down ideas for making it happen If you're handing this off to helpers or wedding party members, leave it to them!

REMEMBER: THIS IS
YOUR WEDDING!

9 IN-PERSON SHOWERS-OF-GIFTS PARTY RESEARCH
Who did you visit? What did you learn, decide, discover, love or hate?

NOTES

10 ATTENDEE LIST
Who's coming to this showers of gifts shindig?

NAME	YES	NO

11 ·····))) LANDING GEAR ENGAGED (((·····

SIZE / QTY / CAPACITY	PRICING NOTES	TIMELINE SPECIFICS

12 FEELING GOOD ABOUT YOUR **SHOWERS-OF-GIFTS PARTY?** READY TO ROCK YOUR WEDDING? **CHECK THAT BOX!** >>> ☐ **COMPLETE!**

's Pre-wedding Party

1 IDENTITY STATEMENT

I am • We are • They are a _____ bride • groom • partner • couple (CIRCLE ONE)
(CIRCLE ONE)   ADJECTIVE   wedding party member • helper

and need a _____ Pre-wedding Party for: _____
                                    ADJECTIVES   CHECKLIST ITEM

that will feel _____
                                    ADJECTIVES, EMOTIONS

and won't _____ or _____ .
                    UNWANTED RESULT, FEELING   UNWANTED RESULT

2 ONLINE RESEARCH   Track the websites you've visited and any initial reactions or discoveries.

IHeartThisWebsiteLikeWhoa.com	Notes on awesomesaucery and other possibilities

3 STYLE + LOOK   List the Pre-wedding Party styles or activities you love. List the things you absolutely despise, too.

LOVE	HATE

4 MaCaW!   What Must, Could, Won't your Pre-wedding Party have or be? Remember: This is YOUR WEDDING.

MUST	COULD	WON'T

5 ENVIRONMENTAL CONDITIONS   What places, weather, or preferences does your Pre-wedding Party need to handle?

6 TIME MACHINE: FAIL   How will you keep things from going wrong?

This **Pre-wedding Party** will fail if:

I will avoid this failure by:

7 TIME MACHINE: SUCCESS   How will you ensure awesomeness and make everything go right?

This **Pre-wedding Party** will succeed if:

I will ensure its success by:

8

GET OUT THERE

If you're planning your own pre-wedding party, use this area to jot down notes for making this party happen. If you're handing this off to helpers or wedding party members, leave it to them!

REMEMBER: THIS IS
YOUR WEDDING!

9 IN-PERSON PRE-WEDDING PARTY RESEARCH

Who did you visit? What did you learn, decide, discover, love or hate?

NOTES

10 ATTENDEE LIST

Who's coming to Partner No. 1's pre-wedding party?

NAME	YES	NO

11 - LANDING GEAR ENGAGED - - - - - - - - - - - - - - - - - - -

SIZE / QTY / CAPACITY	PRICING NOTES	RESERVE-BY SPECIFICS

12 FEELING GOOD ABOUT THAT **PRE-WEDDING PARTY?** READY TO ROCK YOUR WEDDING?   **CHECK THAT BOX!** >>>>   ☐ COMPLETE!

PLAN PARTY BY: ___/___

GUESTS: _____   BUDGET: $_____

PARTNER NO. 2

_____ 's Pre-wedding Party

1 IDENTITY STATEMENT

I am • We are • They are a _____ bride • groom • partner • couple (CIRCLE ONE)
(CIRCLE ONE)   ADJECTIVE   wedding party member • helper

and need a _____ Pre-wedding Party for: _____
                          ADJECTIVES   CHECKLIST ITEM

that will feel _____
                              ADJECTIVES, EMOTIONS

and won't _____ or _____ .
              UNWANTED RESULT, FEELING   UNWANTED RESULT

2 ONLINE RESEARCH   Track the websites you've visited and any initial reactions or discoveries.

IHeartThisWebsiteLikeWhoa.com	Notes on awesomesaucery and other possibilities

3 STYLE + LOOK   List the Pre-wedding Party styles or activities you love. List the things you absolutely despise, too.

LOVE	HATE

4 MaCaW!   What Must, Could, Won't your Pre-wedding Party have or be? Remember: This is YOUR WEDDING.

MUST	COULD	WON'T

5 ENVIRONMENTAL CONDITIONS   What places, weather, or preferences does your Pre-wedding Party need to handle?

6 **TIME MACHINE:** FAIL | How will you keep things from going wrong?

This **Pre-wedding Party** will fail if:

I will avoid this failure by:

7 **TIME MACHINE:** SUCCESS | How will you ensure awesomeness and make everything go right?

This **Pre-wedding Party** will succeed if:

I will ensure its success by:

8

GET OUT THERE

If you're planning your own pre-wedding party, use this area to jot down notes for making this party happen. If you're handing this off to helpers or wedding party members, leave it to them!

REMEMBER: THIS IS

YOUR WEDDING!

9 **IN-PERSON PRE-WEDDING PARTY RESEARCH**

Who did you visit? What did you learn, decide, discover, love or hate?

NOTES

10 **ATTENDEE LIST**

Who's coming to Partner No. 2's pre-wedding party?

NAME	YES	NO

11 - - - - - - - - - - - - - - - - - LANDING GEAR ENGAGED - - - - - - - - - - - - - - - - -

SIZE / QTY / CAPACITY	PRICING NOTES	RESERVE BY SPECIFICS

12 FEELING GOOD ABOUT THAT **PRE-WEDDING PARTY?** READY TO ROCK YOUR WEDDING? | **CHECK THAT BOX!** ➤➤➤➤ | ☐ COMPLETE!

NEED TO DECIDE BY: ___/___

NEED TO HAVE IN HAND BY: ___/___   BUDGET: $_____

Wedding Rings

1 IDENTITY STATEMENT

I am • We are • They are a _____ bride • groom • partner • couple (CIRCLE ONE)
(CIRCLE ONE)   ADJECTIVE   wedding party member • helper

and need to find _____ **Wedding Rings**
                                        ADJECTIVES   CHECKLIST ITEM

that will feel _____
                                        ADJECTIVES, EMOTIONS

and won't _____ or _____.
        UNWANTED RESULT, FEELING   UNWANTED RESULT

2 ONLINE RESEARCH   Track the websites you've visited and any initial reactions or discoveries.

IHeartThisWebsiteLikeWhoa.com	Notes on ring ideas, styles, finishes

3 STYLE + LOOK   List the Wedding Ring styles or looks you love. List the things you absolutely despise, too.

LOVE	HATE

4 MaCaW!   What Must, Could, Won't your Wedding Rings do or provide? Remember: This is YOUR WEDDING.

MUST	COULD	WON'T

5 ENVIRONMENTAL CONDITIONS   What type of activities, work, or lifestyle do your Wedding Rings need to handle?

6 TIME MACHINE: FAIL — How will you keep things from going wrong?

These **Wedding Rings** will fail if:

I will avoid this failure by:

7 TIME MACHINE: SUCCESS — How will you ensure awesomeness and make everything go right?

These **Wedding Rings** will succeed if:

I will ensure their success by:

8

GET OUT THERE

Visit a handful of jewelry stores if that's your thing, talk to your favorite tattoo artist if that's your thing, or have a try-on-a-thon after ordering a bunch of wedding ring options.

REMEMBER: THIS IS
YOUR WEDDING!

9 GET-READY LIST

Prepare to search and shop, or talk with vendors.

BUY / TAKE / ASK / TRY. . .

10 IN-PERSON WEDDING RING RESEARCH

Who did you visit? What did you learn, decide, discover, love or hate?

VENDORS / PLACES VISITED	NOTES

11 ⟩⟩⟩ LANDING GEAR ENGAGED ⟨⟨⟨

RING SIZE NOTES	PRICING NOTES	ORDERING SPECIFICS

12 FEELING GOOD ABOUT YOUR **WEDDING RINGS?** READY TO ROCK YOUR WEDDING? CHECK THAT BOX! ⟩ ⟩ ⟩ ⟩⟩⟩ ☐ COMPLETE!

TRAVEL DATES: ___/___ — ___/___   NEED TO DECIDE BY: ___/___   BUDGET: $_____

1 IDENTITY STATEMENT

I am • We are • They are a _____ bride • groom • partner • couple (CIRCLE ONE)
(CIRCLE ONE)   ADJECTIVE   wedding party member • helper

and need to find a _____ **Honeymoon**
                              ADJECTIVES   CHECKLIST ITEM

that will feel _____
                              ADJECTIVES, EMOTIONS

and won't _____ or _____ .
            UNWANTED RESULT, FEELING   UNWANTED RESULT

2 ONLINE RESEARCH Track the websites you've visited and any initial reactions or discoveries.

IHeartThisWebsiteLikeWhoa.com	Notes on honeymoon awesomesaucery and other ideas

3 STYLE + LOOK List the Honeymoon styles or places you love. List the things you absolutely despise, too.

LOVE	HATE

4 MaCaW! What Must, Could, Won't your Honeymoon do or provide? Remember: This is YOUR WEDDING.

MUST	COULD	WON'T

5 ENVIRONMENTAL CONDITIONS What type of weather and travel does your Honeymoon need to handle?

6 TIME MACHINE: FAIL How will you keep things from going wrong?

Our **Honeymoon** will fail if:

I will avoid this failure by:

7 TIME MACHINE: SUCCESS How will you ensure awesomeness and make everything go right?

Our **Honeymoon** will succeed if:

I will ensure its success by:

8

GET OUT THERE

Plot your course! **Make a list of all the things you want to see and do while celebrating your kickass marriage.** Note any special downtime you want to spend while honeymooning.

REMEMBER: THIS IS
YOUR WEDDING!

9 GET-READY LIST

Prepare to search and shop, or talk with vendors.

BUY / TAKE / ASK / TRY. . .

10 IN-PERSON HONEYMOON RESEARCH

Who did you visit? What did you learn, decide, discover, love or hate?

VENDORS / PLACES VISITED	NOTES

11 - LANDING GEAR ENGAGED -

LENGTH-OF-STAY OPTIONS

PRICING NOTES

BOOKING SPECIFICS

12 FEELING GOOD ABOUT YOUR **HONEYMOON**?
READY TO ROCK YOUR WEDDING?   CHECK THAT BOX! ❯ ❯ ❯❯❯ ☐ COMPLETE!

THINGS TO DO AFTER
YOUR WEDDING

Sift through and choose your favorite photos

You'd be surprised how many photos and how much footage will get taken at your wedding. Sorting through takes time, but it's also an amazing way to celebrate after the fact. Start selecting your favorites for you, your family members, or your guests.

Order prints of photos

Once you've got your favorites, ask your photographer for their print pricing, or try a service like Shutterfly to order the sizes you want.

Order or create a photo album

Put the big day into one big album to have for all time! Apple, Shutterfly, and (hopefully!) your photographer offer great ways to help build the perfect book.

Write thank-you cards

Last but not least, write out those thank-you cards to all your wonderful guests who attended and those who showered you with gifts. A good rule of thumb is to send these out within six months of your wedding date.

GET OUT THERE—

MAKE THIS WEDDING YOURS!

DEPARTMENT	TO-DO CUSTOMIZATION

BLANK WORKSHEETS

USAGE: FOR WHATEVER YA NEED	ACTIVATION CODE: ID02

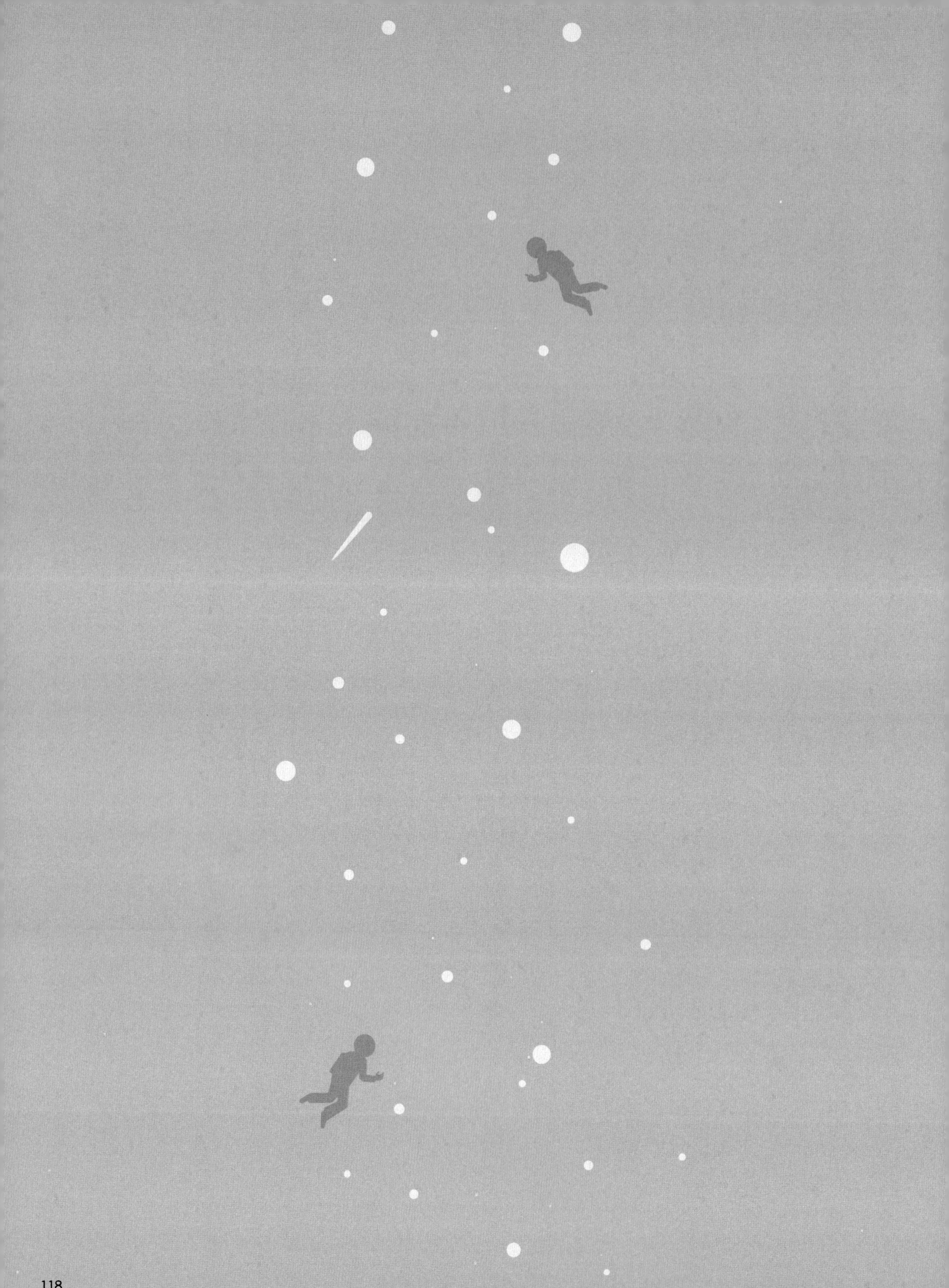

1 IDENTITY STATEMENT

I am • We are • They are a _____ bride • groom • partner • couple (CIRCLE ONE)
(CIRCLE ONE)   ADJECTIVE   wedding party member • helper

and need to find a _____ _____
                                      ADJECTIVES   CHECKLIST ITEM

that will feel _____
                                           ADJECTIVES, EMOTIONS

and won't _____ or _____ .
                 UNWANTED RESULT, FEELING   UNWANTED RESULT

2 ONLINE RESEARCH   Track the websites you've visited and any initial reactions or discoveries.

IHeartThisWebsiteLikeWhoa.com	Notes on why this website's options are great for the big day

3 STYLE + LOOK   List the ideas, styles, or looks you love. List the things you absolutely despise, too.

LOVE	HATE

4 MaCaW!   What things Must, Could, Won't this to-do have or be? Remember: This is YOUR WEDDING.

MUST	COULD	WON'T

5 ENVIRONMENTAL CONDITIONS   What type of weather, people, travel, etc. does this to-do need to handle?

6 TIME MACHINE: FAIL   How will you keep things from going wrong?

This _____ will fail if:

I will avoid this failure by:

7 TIME MACHINE: SUCCESS   How will you ensure awesomeness and make everything go right?

This _____ will succeed if:

I will ensure its success by:

8

GET OUT THERE

Prototype Time: GET UP AND TRY THINGS OUT!
Stand in the place you'll say "I do," test-drive those table favors, and imagine you or your guests celebrating. How does it look? Feel? **Make it YOURS — don't settle!**

REMEMBER: THIS IS
YOUR WEDDING!

9 GET-READY LIST

Prepare to search and shop or talk with vendors.

BUY / TAKE / ASK / TRY...

10 VENDOR / IN-STORE RESEARCH

Who did you visit? What did you learn, decide, discover, love or hate?

VENDORS / PLACES VISITED	NOTES

11 ----------- ((⊁)) LANDING GEAR ENGAGED ((⊁)) -----------

SIZE / QTY / CAPACITY	PRICING NOTES PRICE BREAKS, SHIPPING, ETC.	ORDER / RESERVE-BY SPECIFICS

12 FEELING GOOD ABOUT YOUR DECISION?
READY TO ROCK YOUR WEDDING?   CHECK THAT BOX! ❯ ❯ ❯❯   ☐ COMPLETE!

NEED TO DECIDE BY: ___/___   GUESTS: _____   BUDGET: $_____

To-Do: _____

1 IDENTITY STATEMENT

I am • We are • They are a _____ bride • groom • partner • couple (CIRCLE ONE)
(CIRCLE ONE)   ADJECTIVE   wedding party member • helper

and need to find a _____ _____
                              ADJECTIVES   CHECKLIST ITEM

that will feel _____
                              ADJECTIVES, EMOTIONS

and won't _____ or _____.
                UNWANTED RESULT, FEELING   UNWANTED RESULT

2 ONLINE RESEARCH   Track the websites you've visited and any initial reactions or discoveries.

IHeartThisWebsiteLikeWhoa.com	Notes on why this website's options are great for the big day

3 STYLE + LOOK   List the ideas, styles, or looks you love. List the things you absolutely despise, too.

LOVE	HATE

4 MaCaW!   What things *Must, Could, Won't* this to-do have or be? Remember: This is YOUR WEDDING.

MUST	COULD	WON'T

5 ENVIRONMENTAL CONDITIONS   What type of weather, people, travel, etc. does this to-do need to handle?

6 TIME MACHINE: FAIL   How will you keep things from going wrong?

This _____ will fail if:

I will avoid this failure by:

7 TIME MACHINE: SUCCESS   How will you ensure awesomeness and make everything go right?

This _____ will succeed if:

I will ensure its success by:

8

GET OUT THERE

Prototype Time: GET UP AND TRY THINGS OUT!
Stand in the place you'll say "I do," test-drive those table favors, and imagine you or your guests celebrating. How does it look? Feel? **Make it YOURS — don't settle!**

REMEMBER: THIS IS
YOUR WEDDING!

9 GET-READY LIST
Prepare to search and shop or talk with vendors.

BUY / TAKE / ASK / TRY...

10 VENDOR / IN-STORE RESEARCH
Who did you visit? What did you learn, decide, discover, love or hate?

VENDORS / PLACES VISITED	NOTES

11 -------- (((LANDING GEAR ENGAGED (((--------

SIZE / QTY / CAPACITY	PRICING NOTES PRICE BREAKS, SHIPPING, ETC.	ORDER / RESERVE-BY SPECIFICS

12 FEELING GOOD ABOUT YOUR DECISION?
READY TO ROCK YOUR WEDDING?   CHECK THAT BOX! ⟩ ⟩ ⟩ ⟩   ☐ COMPLETE!

NEED TO DECIDE BY: ___/___   GUESTS: _____   BUDGET: $_____

To-Do: _____

1 IDENTITY STATEMENT

I am • We are • They are a _____ bride • groom • partner • couple (CIRCLE ONE)
(CIRCLE ONE)   ADJECTIVE   wedding party member • helper

and need to find a _____ _____
                                ADJECTIVES   CHECKLIST ITEM

that will feel _____
                                    ADJECTIVES, EMOTIONS

and won't _____ or _____.
                UNWANTED RESULT, FEELING   UNWANTED RESULT

2 ONLINE RESEARCH Track the websites you've visited and any initial reactions or discoveries.

IHeartThisWebsiteLikeWhoa.com	Notes on why this website's options are great for the big day

3 STYLE + LOOK List the ideas, styles, or looks you <u>love</u>. List the things you <u>absolutely despise</u>, too.

LOVE	HATE

4 MaCaW! What things *Must*, *Could*, *Won't* this to-do have or be? Remember: This is YOUR WEDDING.

MUST	COULD	WON'T

5 ENVIRONMENTAL CONDITIONS What type of weather, people, travel, etc. does this to-do need to handle?

6 TIME MACHINE: FAIL How will you keep things from going wrong?

This _____ will fail if:

I will avoid this failure by:

7 TIME MACHINE: SUCCESS How will you ensure awesomeness and make everything go right?

This _____ will succeed if:

I will ensure its success by:

8

GET OUT THERE

Prototype Time: GET UP AND TRY THINGS OUT!
Stand in the place you'll say "I do," test-drive those table favors, and imagine you or your guests celebrating. How does it look? Feel? **Make it YOURS — don't settle!**

REMEMBER: THIS IS
YOUR WEDDING!

9 GET-READY LIST
Prepare to search and shop or talk with vendors.

BUY / TAKE / ASK / TRY...

10 VENDOR / IN-STORE RESEARCH
Who did you visit? What did you learn, decide, discover, love or hate?

VENDORS / PLACES VISITED	NOTES

11 ╾ LANDING GEAR ENGAGED ╼

SIZE / QTY / CAPACITY	PRICING NOTES PRICE BREAKS, SHIPPING, ETC.	ORDER / RESERVE-BY SPECIFICS

12 FEELING GOOD ABOUT YOUR DECISION? READY TO ROCK YOUR WEDDING? **CHECK THAT BOX!** ⟫ ⟫ ⟫ ☐ **COMPLETE!**

NEED TO DECIDE BY: __/__ GUESTS: _____ BUDGET: $_____

To-Do: _____

1 IDENTITY STATEMENT

I am • We are • They are a _____ bride • groom • partner • couple (CIRCLE ONE)
(CIRCLE ONE)   ADJECTIVE   wedding party member • helper

and need to find a _____ _____
                              ADJECTIVES   CHECKLIST ITEM

that will feel _____
                          ADJECTIVES, EMOTIONS

and won't _____ or _____.
          UNWANTED RESULT, FEELING   UNWANTED RESULT

2 ONLINE RESEARCH Track the websites you've visited and any initial reactions or discoveries.

IHeartThisWebsiteLikeWhoa.com	Notes on why this website's options are great for the big day

3 STYLE + LOOK List the ideas, styles, or looks you love. List the things you absolutely despise, too.

LOVE	HATE

4 MaCaW! What things Must, Could, Won't this to-do have or be? Remember: This is YOUR WEDDING.

MUST	COULD	WON'T

5 ENVIRONMENTAL CONDITIONS What type of weather, people, travel, etc. does this to-do need to handle?

6 TIME MACHINE: FAIL   How will you keep things from going wrong?

This _____ will fail if:

I will avoid this failure by:

7 TIME MACHINE: SUCCESS   How will you ensure awesomeness and make everything go right?

This _____ will succeed if:

I will ensure its success by:

---

8 GET OUT THERE

Prototype Time: GET UP AND TRY THINGS OUT!
Stand in the place you'll say "I do," test-drive those table favors, and imagine you or your guests celebrating. How does it look? Feel? **Make it YOURS — don't settle!**

REMEMBER: THIS IS
YOUR WEDDING!

9 GET-READY LIST
Prepare to search and shop or talk with vendors.

BUY / TAKE / ASK / TRY...

10 VENDOR / IN-STORE RESEARCH
Who did you visit? What did you learn, decide, discover, love or hate?

VENDORS / PLACES VISITED	NOTES

11))) LANDING GEAR ENGAGED (((

SIZE / QTY / CAPACITY	PRICING NOTES PRICE BREAKS, SHIPPING, ETC.	ORDER / RESERVE-BY SPECIFICS

12 FEELING GOOD ABOUT YOUR DECISION? READY TO ROCK YOUR WEDDING?   CHECK THAT BOX! >>> □ COMPLETE!

1 IDENTITY STATEMENT

I am • We are • They are a _____ bride • groom • partner • couple (CIRCLE ONE)
(CIRCLE ONE)   ADJECTIVE   wedding party member • helper

and need to find a _____ _____
                              ADJECTIVES   CHECKLIST ITEM

that will feel _____
                         ADJECTIVES, EMOTIONS

and won't _____ or _____.
              UNWANTED RESULT, FEELING   UNWANTED RESULT

2 ONLINE RESEARCH   Track the websites you've visited and any initial reactions or discoveries.

IHeartThisWebsiteLikeWhoa.com	Notes on why this website's options are great for the big day

3 STYLE + LOOK   List the ideas, styles, or looks you love. List the things you absolutely despise, too.

LOVE	HATE

4 MaCaW!   What things *Must, Could, Won't* this to-do have or be? Remember: This is YOUR WEDDING.

MUST	COULD	WON'T

5 ENVIRONMENTAL CONDITIONS   What type of weather, people, travel, etc. does this to-do need to handle?

6 **TIME MACHINE:** FAIL   How will you keep things from going wrong?

This _____ will fail if:

I will avoid this failure by:

7 **TIME MACHINE:** SUCCESS   How will you ensure awesomeness and make everything go right?

This _____ will succeed if:

I will ensure its success by:

8

GET OUT THERE

Prototype Time: GET UP AND TRY THINGS OUT!
Stand in the place you'll say "I do," test-drive those table favors, and imagine you or your guests celebrating. How does it look? Feel? **Make it YOURS — don't settle!**

REMEMBER: THIS IS
YOUR WEDDING!

9 **GET-READY LIST**

Prepare to search and shop or talk with vendors.

BUY / TAKE / ASK / TRY . . .

10 **VENDOR / IN-STORE RESEARCH**

Who did you visit? What did you learn, decide, discover, love or hate?

VENDORS / PLACES VISITED	NOTES

11))) LANDING GEAR ENGAGED (((

SIZE / QTY / CAPACITY	PRICING NOTES PRICE BREAKS, SHIPPING, ETC.	ORDER / RESERVE-BY SPECIFICS

12 FEELING GOOD ABOUT YOUR DECISION? READY TO ROCK YOUR WEDDING?   CHECK THAT BOX! ▶ ⟫ ⟫⟫ ☐ COMPLETE!

MORE SPACEY PRODUCTS

TO HELP YOUR WEDDING PLANNING KICK MAJOR ASS

COLLECT THEM ALL!

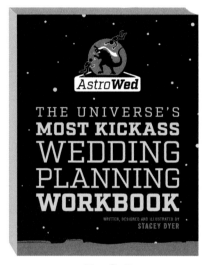

Book 1

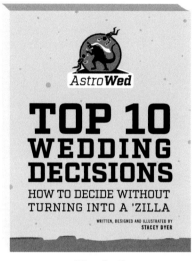

Book 2

Book 3

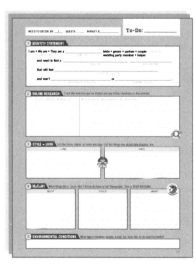

**Blank
Worksheets**

**Priority
Galaxies**

And much, much more!

Visit Astro-Wed.com and find us on these fine social platforms:

@AstroWedHQ

Made in the
USA
Middletown, DE